COMMUNICATION AS A MANAGEMENT TOOL

COMMUNICATION
AS A
MANAGEMENT TOOL

Adarsh Kumar Varma

Foreword by
Prof. Mukund Lal

Guest Chapters by
Anil Ambani
Gurcharan Das

Publications

KALPAZ PUBLICATIONS
Delhi - 110052

Communication as a Management Tool

ISBN : 81-7835-586-8

Rs. 690

Published in 2007 in India by
Kalpaz Publications
C-30, Satyawati Nagar,
Delhi - 110052
e-mail : kalpaz@hotmail.com

Laser Typesetting at : Vinayak Printers, Delhi
Printed at : Salasar Imaging System, Delhi

Contents

GUEST CHAPTERS

MEMOS FOR MANAGEMENT

Foreword

A number of books on the various aspects of communication have been written and published by Indian authors so far, but I am glad to find that Prof. Adarsh Kumar Varma's present book on *Communication As A Management Tool* is unique in many significant respects worth appreciation, whether we evaluate it from the point of view of its content or from the point of view of the presentation of the different paradigms of the subject. The main quality of the book is its originality of approach followed by a deeper spirit of professionalism displayed from the beginning to the end–a quality which is hard to find in a book of this calibre.

The book is divided into 20 chapters all of which are exhaustive, but everywhere the discussion is precise, to the point and heart-catching. The first 15 chapters are related to the 'Symbiotic Relationship', whereas the other chapters are devoted to the exposition of Business Communication. In each of these chapters, the ideas and thoughts on the topics under study have been so clearly and vividly portrayed and highlighted that they create a lasting effect on the minds of the readers. Not only this, the examples quoted by the author for clarifying his views are so homely and appealing that even the complex ideologies and concepts requiring deeper mental exercise to understand can be easily understood by the readers in their proper context.

The book is also an extraordinary piece of the author's contribution as demonstrated by its literary approach. Throughout, he appears to be familiar with the great works of English literature as also the world-class events of political, economic, social and psychological importance in which so many important personalities had played a significant role through their communication power and communication skill or had suffered serious consequences as a result of communication failures or communication gaps or other communication barriers. The examples from the business scenario in India as also those of the world add a further flavour to the author's way of writing and addressing the readers to understand the strength of communication as a basic tool of management. Besides, many of the brilliant examples based on his experience in the field of journalism add further fragrance to his flowering approach and strengthen his clarity of thoughts and the vivid exposition of his precious talent for enriching the knowledge of the readers who sincerely desire to have a powerful command over the art and science of communication as a tool of management.

Whatever has been remarked above about the author's splendid contribution is also found fully authenticated in respect of his chapters on Business Communication. All the chapters on this topic are full of brilliant examples of the significant business writing and business reports with which the author himself had been personally associated in one way or the other as a prolific journalist of great repute. So all discussions in these chapters are not only homely and interesting, they also provide ample opportunity to the readers to understand the nature and purpose and appropriate designing and layout of such reports as also their role in polishing and strengthening the business communication networks on which the real success of our business depends. Further, an excellent and thought-providing article *When Less is More* by a senior management personality of our country, Mr. Gurcharan Das, is going to add a new golden feather to Prof. Varma's cap.

There is no denying the fact that the present book will definitely provide our professionals a vibratory and pragmatic armour to face the challenges posed before them by the various bottlenecks of communication that they are expected to face in this new millennium which are expected to make their task of achieving the missions, goals and objectives so difficult and sometimes even unfathomable. They are, in my opinion, going to be largely benefited if they make it a point to concentrate on and keep themselves faithfully guided by the noble ideas and the intellectual approach presented by the author in this precious book.

After a thorough evaluation of the rich material contained herein, I find myself fully convinced that Prof. Varma's unbound majesty of thoughts so painstakingly and vividly portrayed will go a long way in not only enlightening our management students and business professionals associated with various business and industrial organizations, but will also prove to be a permanent asset to them in life in sharpening their communication skills and widening the frontiers of knowledge in the field of information technology and mass communication so as to discharge their duties and responsibilities as per the need of the environmental changes.

My Congratulations!

School of Management Sciences
Khushipur,
Varansi.

Mukund Lal
Director

Preface

The Story Behind This Book

When a management institute invited me to teach *Communication for Management* to M.B.A. students, the idea made sense to me. I had been a journalist and a teacher of the subject for four decades. I also had extensive man-management experience, having been the Editor of three publications and the Head of the Department of News Agency Journalism.

To brush up my knowledge of the subject. I went to various libraries. Some of the things to be covered in the course were found in some books but not in others, other things were to be found in other books. More than a dozen books had to be consulted. How could one expect a student to consult a dozen books on just one subject ?

At first, I wrote out what I would cover in a particular lecture. The write-ups came out fine, so I sent them for publication. They were accepted. I wrote further, and finally decided it had to be planned methodically so that there would be a single book that the student could treat as a benchmark. If he wanted to go deeper into a particular topic, he could always go to the library.

This is how *Communication As A Management Tool* was born.

To make it methodical and easy for the student to understand, the book has been divided into three parts. The first part, consisting of 15 chapters, describes how the relationship between communication and management is symbiotic. Of these chapters, the first four detail how communication works and how it is related to management, including the roles of the communicator, the receiver of communication, encoding and decoding.

Chapter 5 tells why time management and fixing priorities are crucial. Chapter 6 describes how excellence in management goes into the making of a brand. When a brand is successful, its clout means there is money value in it. The brand can consequently be sold and bought all by itself without any tangible asset changing hands with it.

The next chapter deals with the crucial role of vision in management. Thomas Alva Edison, in his time the holder of the largest number of patents in the world, was just one of the thousands of physicists of his time. But he had a vision. Dhirubhai Ambani was a petrol pump attendant at one time. But he had a vision, so he founded the world's largest crude oil refinery which is feeding thousands of petrol pumps. Going further, he developed the largest business empire in the history of India. It was so big that even after partition between his two sons, each of the two entities is a titan.

There are different patterns of communication used by different mangers. JRD Tata followed one, Russi Modi another. Dhirubhai Ambani used his own unique pattern. Brij Mohan Lal Munjal devised his own strategy. All of them were successful. There is really no "right" or "wrong" pattern of communication. The acid test is whether your pattern works. If it does, it is the right pattern for your situation.

However, there are five mandatory *mantras* of management that have evolved over time. It has been found that all managers have to religiously follow these *mantras* if they are to be successful.

When the first draft of the manuscript was almost ready, Anil Ambani wrote an article in the *Times of India* telling how Dhirubhai Ambani's vision led to the business version of Log Cabin to White House. It has been used as Guest Chapter I courtesy the *Times of India.*

The second part, consisting of four chapters, concentrates on the complexities of business communication. Specifically, it describes the different kinds of routine, periodical and special reports which keep the wheels of business moving.

The book has been fashioned on the pattern of IGNOU's learning units. Each chapter is followed by a summary with a few self-check exercises at the end. To enable the student to verify how right he was in answering them, Chapter 20 gives model answers with which he can check his own answers.

The third part is a guest chapter by Mr. Gurcharan Das, the famous management expert. I was going to write about the role memos play in business management when Mr. Gurcharan Das wrote an excellent piece on the topic in the *Times of India*. Seeing no point in re-inventing the wheel, and certain that I couldn't write it better than him, I sought permission to use it as Guest Chapter 2. He granted permission and advised me to credit it to the *Times of India.* Here is thanking both Mr. Gurcharan Das and the *Times of India.*

Adarsh Kumar Varma

Acknowledgements

How Many Thanks? To How Many?

It was a distinctly Varanasi-esque atmosphere in which I taught *Communication for Management* to MBA students. The Director of the Institute, Prof. Vinod Batura, was from Varanasi. The Registrar, Dr. Saxena, and the Professor who briefed me, Dr. Taruna, had the aura of laid back erudition typical of Varanasi. It suited me, steeped in Varanasi culture as I am, having been raised in that holiest of holy cities.

I made demands which Guest Faculty almost never make, like giving me three continuous classes in which one could combine a lecture with practical exercises to be done by the students. In a professional course nothing can replace a do-it-yourself stint.

The Varanasi touch continued. Cartoonist Dhir, whom I have known since he was a young man (I was also young then, by the way, though not that young), dropped in when he learned that I was teaching there. I took him to meet the Director. To my surprise, they greeted each other like long lost friends! They apparently knew each other from their Varanasi days.

Dhir brought another Varanasi touch to the study that was ultimately to become this book. One look at the manuscript, and he took it upon himself to get a Foreword written by Prof. Mukund Lal.

It so happens that Prof. Mukund Lal, now Director of the School of Management Sciences, Khushipur (Varanasi), had been the Dean of the Faculty of Management Studies at Banaras Hindu University before opting to found the ambitious Khushipur institution. Among his students are Directors and Professors at management institutes.

What luck for this Guru of Gurus to recommend this book!

Profuse thanks to Dhir, Prof. Mukund Lal, Prof. Vinod Batura, Dr. Saxena and Dr. Taruna.

I must thank Amit Garg, the man who is publishing this book. The Gargs are in a majority nowhere, but like the Sikhs they are in the driver's seat wherever they are. It is said that if India's moon mission sends a man to that earth satellite, he will find Indian food there served by a Sardarji running a tandoor. Amit's only problem will be that no Garg has ever manned a tandoor, not at least to my knowledge.

Adarsh Kumar Varma

PART I

A SYMBIOTIC RELATIONSHIP

1

Crusoe, His Man Friday and the Message of the Gun

Robinson Crusoe needed no communication until he found another human being. The moment this happened, the two felt the need to communicate with each other. The first thing that Crusoe did was to indicate to the man, by gestures and sounds, that he had nothing to fear, and that they could, and would, be friends. He also taught the man that his name was Friday. Crusoe named himself Master and made the man understand all this without the facility of a common language. The two, as we know, managed famously with each others.

Communication and management go together. Without communication there can be no management.

How Communication

Communication is the art of making oneself understood. It is not merely speaking a message or making a gesture. However, understanding includes misunderstanding, just as action includes wrong action. When Bertie Wooster indicated to Jeeves, by word or action, that the time for whisky and soda had come, Jeeves brought the drink. But supposing he interpreted the words and /or gestures to mean that the master wanted Jeeves to pour a drink for himself (which he did not)? He might have misunderstood but the communication had been made.

Communication can be by words, gestures (as Crusoe and Friday managed), body language and/or other means, Crusoe must have communicated through body language, gestures and assertive behavior who was master and who had to carry our instructions.

In short, you cannot not communicate.

Crusoe's gun, which scared away the cannibals who were about to kill and eat Friday, must also have communicated a message. The message was that Crusoe had the power to be boss. Man and horse have lived together in this world for ages. Yet man rides horse, horse never rides man. The reason is that man has communicated to horse, and communicates to every horse since he was a foal, who is master and who must carry out instructions.

The manner of dressing and carrying oneself also communicates a message. One cannot dress like a tramp and yet expect to be considered boss. Look around and you will find that the well-groomed man usually has his way whereas someone dressed in rags and with straggling hair and worn out shoes has to struggle to gain entry and acceptance in society. The only man who gains entry in fashionable Indian society barefoot is MF Hussain. But Hussain's bare feet too convey a message, the message of a man who considers himself a genius and doesn't care for society. Further, according to him, society must care for him since he is a genius.

'Think British'

Despite Hussain, however, appearance does count. Here is a real life example. When elected governments were formed in the Indian provinces in 1946 after the war, the British companies which dominated the Indian commercial scene did a quick think.

So far they had to deal with ICS and IP officers who were British. Even the stray Indian who made it to these hallowed cadres behaved and dressed like Englishmen, suit, tie and all, and even contrived a British pronunciation and accent. As Lord Macaulay had prescribed a century earlier, they tried very hard to be like Englishmen and "think British".

The British companies which did business with the provincial and central governments were all headed by Britons. The managing directors, the directors and most of those who wielded power, including those who had to go out to the Secretariat to swing deals, contracts, etc, were also British. They had to deal with fellow Britons who were Secretaries to the government and manned all the senior positions. Both sets of negotiators talked on the same wave length. However, while the nitty gritty of deals were negotiated by the officials on the two sides, in the new situation the big "yes's" and "no's" had to come from the *dhoti*-clad ministers.

If there was one thing that Mahatma Gandhi had taught his followers, it was irreverence for authority and for the white skin. So the ministers headed by Govind Ballabh Pant in U.P. had to be humoured if deals were to be swung.

Backroom Boys

How to do it? In between the top brass and the field officers who negotiated, there was a cadre of backroom boys in the companies who were also called officers and got fat salaries and perks like other officers. They were mostly Indian and worked out the terms on which deals could be made. They also worked out other details and knew everything about the manner in which the companies did business.

What the British companies did was to change this. The backroom boys, though ethnic Indians, were well groomed in British ways of thinking, behaviour and speaking. The companies put them in field jobs and the largely British field staff were assigned backroom work. The calculation was that the *dhoti*-clad ministers would be more comfortable dealing with Indian representatives of British companies.

The calculation was fine except for one detail. The British companies had not reckoned with the Indian peons and *babus*. Trained to be deferential to the white skin, the peons and *babus* had been putting no hurdles in the way of the white company officials when they came to meet big government officers. Now, with the brown skin Indians representing the companies, all kinds of entry restrictions became common. Some examples of the hurdles which they faced all of us are familiar with –"*Saheb* is at a meeting", or "time to meet *Saheb* is from 11 a.m. to 1 p.m."

The companies learnt fast. They put back the Indians into the backroom and reinstated the Britons as company representatives. Business flowed again unhindered. This is what mere "appearance" can do!

Incidentally, when I went to Lucknow as Editor of the *Pioneer*, I was told that the Editor of the *Pioneer* always stayed with the Viceroy when he went to Delhi in the "good old days". The man who told me this in 1985 was Dr. S.N. Ghosh, who had become the first Indian Editor of the paper way back in 1946. He had retired in 1972 but had been retained as Advisor.

Verbal Communication

We have in the above paragraphs made an effort to learn of how gestures, grooming and appearance communicate messages. But the commonest medium of communication is *verbal*, that is through language. Verbal communication can be *oral* or *written*.

Oral communication has its advantages and disadvantages. It is faster, which is an advantage. But it can be inaccurate or incomplete. X says "follow me". Y may do so, but only an hour later, while X wanted him to be immediately behind him. Napoleon asked Marshal Nye to position his army at a particular place. He did not specify that he was about to launch an offensive immediately and Nye should follow the instruction immediately. Nye tarried to give his fagged out troops rest. The result was Waterloo.

Sir Winston Churchill records in his War Memoirs that during the initial years of World War II, General Wavell as GOC-in-C, Middle East, put up a valiant fight against Field-Marshal Rommel's Afrika Korps, but his army was badly outgunned and outmanned and he had to order retreat after retreat. To give him respite and to raise morale, Churchill posted him back to India as Viceroy since his military expertise and experience were needed to stem the Japanese advance on India through South-East Asia.

Auchinleck's Misunderstanding

Simultaneously he reinforced the Middle-East army with many Indian and some Australian troops, sent more guns and tanks and posted General Auchinleck as GOC-in-C with orders to attack. The idea was to thwart Rommel's plans to capture the Suez route to India even though the British Indian force was not yet powerful enough to roll him back. Auchinleck proceeded to make his own assessment and found that he was still outgunned and outmanned, so he sent a long list of the tanks, guns, aircraft and men he required in order to attack. Chrchill, quickly realizing that Auchinleck had misunderstood his mission, posted Auchinleck back to India as Commander-in Chief and replaced him in the Middle-East with Montgomery, who won the famous battle of El Alamein. Either Churchill's orders were unclear or Auchinleck had misunderstood them.

Closer to our time, Brig. Surender Singh, commanding the Kargil sector, was ordered to carry out reconnaissance to find out the extent of the enemy's penetration. The unstated message was to use the men he had. He, however, apparently thought it was his duty to estimate and report how this was to be done. He asked for unmanned aerial reconnaissance vehicles and more troops to carry out the chore. He was replaced because, in Army Headquarters' thinking, he had misunderstood his mission. His successor was asked to get on with the job even as reinforcements were sent.

Written Communication

Written communication has the advantage of being more specific. It may take time to draft and convey, but the chances of misunderstanding are markedly lower. Besides, the recipient can revert to the written message once, twice or more times to make sure he is following it.

Facial expression, posture, the display of confidence or lack of it are other important forms of non-verbal communication. Consider the following simple sentence:

What were you doing last night?

Said with a frown, it conveys a different message from the time it is said with a smile. The same question asked on the telephone may be interpreted differently since gestures and facial expressions cannot be conveyed on the telephone. However, the tone and the pitch of the voice, threatening or soothing, loud or low, can make the communication carry different messages.

Non-Verbal Messages

Yet, some non-verbal messages have unique advantages. Traffic signals and signs on the road convey their message far more effectively, cheaply and efficiently than the posting of a constable to convey the same message can do. A man warning of a sharp turning at a dead end is likely to miss many more cars and other vehicles during peak traffic hours than a traffic sign. This is apart from the fact that a man warning of a sharp turning at a dead end is likely to slow down traffic greatly.

Even silence can be used to convey a meaning. At independence in 1947 each princely state had the option of acceeding either to India or to Pakistan. Many princes had doubts and made a written representation. Some made a beeline for Delhi. Sardar Patel arranged to meet them in a big conference hall. He studied the representations and made a mental note of what he was to say to whom.

As he entered the hall, the princes stood up. He gestured to them to sit down, then moved from table to table clarifying the doubt of each prince individually. One prince had made a written representation how his ancestors had earned the right to rule in perpetuity through valour. When Patel came to his table, he stood up to propound his theory. Patel, told by his aides who he was, remembered his theory of the right to rule in perpetuity. Even as the prince was expounding his theory, Patel moved on. Not a word in reply. The prince got the message, returned to his state and signed the instrument of accession.

'No Decision' Communication

No decision is also a decision in certain cases. A senior Government official I know tried in 1960 to pull political strings to get an extension on the eve of retirement. He spoke to MPs and MLAs and even found a channel to approach the concerned minister. On the day of retirement he phoned his contact man in the capital. The contact man told him the minister had gone that morning on tour without taking a decision. The official understood the message and handed over charge to his successor.

For illiterate audiences the sign frequently conveys the message for which written communication and oral persuasion prove inadequate. The inverted red triangle for family planning is an example. Another example is the skull and crossbones signifying danger. At some electrical installations we find the notice *Danger* 2000 volts. But it can only be effective for those who can read and, further, know enough of physics to realize what 2000 volts means. For the illiterate, or for those to whom 2000 volts is Greek, it can be like any other graffiti on the urinal wall in an alien language.

One ingredient of communication that the communicator dare not miss is the context and relevance. The question *What were you doing last night?* is relevant in certain contexts and not relevant in others.

You are traveling on the road and stop a stranger and ask *What were you doing last night?* The stranger will be perfectly justified in giving you a rude reply, like *Mind your own business* or *What right do you have to ask this question?* He might even push you aside and go his way. Or, if he is in a bad mood, he might even punch you.

When Question Becomes Relevant

But the question becomes relevant when asked by a police officer investigating a crime on the relevant night. If he has reason to suspect that the man did something connected with the crime, or himself committed the crime, that night, he has a right to ask this question and expect a reply. Similarly, a spouse may be justified in asking this question if s/he has a reason to suspect that her/his partner was guilty of an act of infidelity.

All of us know that the bulk of the judgment in a court case is devoted to the context. The judgment first states the differing versions of the parties, defines the dispute, then summarizes the arguments of the parties. The court's verdict comes towards the end, giving reasons for arriving at the conclusion.

Noting in Files

This is necessary since the judgement in a court case is supposed to be so complete a document that one need not make further inquiries to find out what the dispute was about and what the verdict is.

Similarly, notings in official files try to be as complete a statement of the case as possible. Towards the end of his initial note, the junior official may list the various options available to the decision-maker in the case. The decision maker, who may be a senior official or politician authorized to take the decision, may thereupon give his verdict in a few words or a few sentences.

He may even write a laconic " complaint dismissed. Parties may be informed." This is because the context is already stated in the junior official's noting. Anyone reading such a note will understand without difficulty what the case was about and what the decision is.

A Complete Whole

It is for this reason that each judgement and each office note pertaining to a case is supposed to be a complete whole giving the whole context and the verdict.

But court cases and official decisions, while grabbing newspaper headlines in some cases, form but a part of human interaction. A shot in a film may just show the big man shouting "you are dismissed" to the underling. The film-maker need not make the big boss give reasons in detail for the dismissal since the reasons are clear from the sequence of events shown earlier.

Outside films also, one frequently finds a person saying "congratulations" to another person, or reprimanding him without giving any reason. The reason is that, in such situations, both parties know the context.

SUMMING UP

Management is the art of getting things done. Communication is the art of getting one's message understood. Unless the manager gets himself understood, he cannot get things done.

Communication can be verbal or non-verbal. Verbal is through language, and can be either oral (spoken word) or written, or a combination of the two.

Non-verbal communication can be through gestures, posture, facial expression, sign language, or even through silence or non-decision.

Self-Check Exercises

1. An employee applies for casual leave for the next day in an organization in which leave cannot be availed of unless it is sanctioned. He receives no sanction. Can he avail of the leave? If not, why?

   (Space for answer)

2. Cite an example from your experience of silence as communication.

   (Space for answer)

2

Vertical and Horizontal, Upward and Downward Communication

The situation in which one is expected to manage others comes when one heads some kind of organization or campaign. It can be an office, a factory, a sales team, a military unit or even a voluntary organization dedicated to, say, keeping a locality free of garbage. While there will be nuanced differences between different classes of cases, some principles are applicable to all.

In every situation in which an individual or a group is detailed to manage a body of men, there will be *vertical* and *horizontal* communication. Vertical communication can be *upwards* or *downwards*. Downward communication is considered by the laity as the essence of vertical communication since in many cases it comes in the shape of orders or instructions. But let us be warned that upward communication plays a significant role in determining success or failure. Typically, downward communication takes the shape of the boss barking orders, oral or written. It can be *chain* or *cluster* communication. That is, the boss issuing orders to a sub-boss or sub-bosses, who then either pass them further down or try to implement them.

Language of the Order

An order by the boss can be a one-sentence thing telling what is expected to be achieved in what time frame. More often, it is a complicated thing telling not merely of what is expected to be achieved. Sometimes it is couched in technical jargon, which is all right if the person or persons to whom it is addressed understand it. Sometimes legalese is used. The smart manager will keep in mind not his own level of knowledge but the level of knowledge and literacy of those who receive such communication.

Frequently the hurdle is not technical knowledge but knowledge of the language, more specially in a country like India where the mother tongue of the sub-bosses and workers is different from the language of the boss. While even the lower level staff may understand the technical terms, the purport of the order may elude them. Consider the following:

> *A district magistrate of an administrative area inhabited by members of different religious communities issues instructions that executive and police officers should discourage people of one religious persuasion from entering areas inhabited by people of a different religious persuasion at night. Within an area where people of one religious persuasion predominate, an eye should be kept on inordinately large confluences of people, specially when planning to, or moving, at odd hours, towards areas where small groups of non-conforming people are bunched together.*

What does it mean to the *daroga* or the constable? One of them may decipher it to mean that crowds are banned at night and should be dispersed by force if necessary. Another may decide that any crowd at any time is to be dispersed. A third may do nothing, contending that there are no specific orders to restrain anyone from doing anything. He will move only when there is a breach of the law, and then he will use force. Only the very perceptive will understand that it means increased vigilance and the spreading of informers to keep the police abreast of what is happening or planned.

The whole idea of issuing this order is to prevent a breach of the peace. If a law or the public peace is broken, there is no need for a pre-emptive order by the district magistrate. The police and the magistracy of the area have standing orders on what to do.

An example of a *cluster* downward communication is a circular. It is issued to, say, managers of all departments of a factory, or the station house officers of all the police stations. Circulars have to be couched in general terms since they do not deal with a specific situation.

Cluster Communication

A circular saying that all workers must become operational at reporting time is a reminder to everyone of his duty. For those who report for work on time and do become operational, it is a polite exhortation to keep it up. It may even be construed as a pat on the back.

For others it is a reminder that they have not done their complete duty when they report on time. They must become operational also. Finally, it is a veiled warning to those who come on time and then adjourn to the canteen for tea and gossip.

Downward communication can also consist of information, though it is usually accompanied by instructions. When Gujarat was engulfed in riots for more than a month, everyone knew of it through the media. But officials in neighbouring states, more specially in districts contiguous with Gujarat, must have alerted their law enforcing authorities about what was going on in their immediate neighbourhood.

This must have been accompanied by instructions on the measures to be taken to prevent the infection from seeping in. Whether they did do so is not known, but it was expected of them. In such situations it does not do to depend upon local officials to learn from media reports.

Media coverage

The media frequently do not cover events where enough is not "new", for let us remember that one of the components of news in newness, if not the main component. A factory making glazed tiles for bathrooms may be one of half a dozen in a country. If two or three or four of them have to restrict production because of power shortage, the higher management would most likely take note, for to keep an eye on the demand and supply situation is part of its main functions.

Different Focus

The individual factory may not take note of this development, for its focus is on the optimum use of resources and facilities to produce tiles of the requisite quality at a competitive cost. Its workers almost certainly, and the management very likely, are not keeping an eye on the supply situation.

As for the media, curtailed production because of erratic power supply in isolated cases is not one of the priority areas to cover, though if a factory is burnt down or destroyed in any other way the media are likely to notice this. In this situation an alert from the higher management about the deteriorating supply position, which can mean higher and more urgent demand for the produce of the factory, and possibly higher prices, should be expected. There can also be suggestions from the higher management about how the factory should go about making adjustments to meet the emerging situation.

Business Establishments

Business establishments are not sleeping behemoths like Government offices which, once established, continue to follow a certain procedure like automatons until an iconoclast or a saboteur throws a spanner in the works. Secondly, unlike Government offices which have a monopoly of whatever they do, business is subject to intense and day-to-day competition. A reduction in import duty on cement will put domestic producers under pressure and cut into their margin. An increase in excise duty will exert similar pressure. A rise in demand on a resurgence of construction activity will exert a different kind of pressure.

First, the cement company may be expected to increase production even at short notice to meet the increasing demand. However, this will directly benefit the company since higher production from the same infrastructure means higher per unit profit, for which primarily the company was formed.

Secondly, a rise in demand usually results in higher prices in a free market, which is enough of an incentive for any commercial concern.

Things like an increase or decrease in import or export duty, a rise in demand, or an increase or decrease in excise duty are the concern of the corporate office of a company. Consequently, there is a flurry of downward communication from it to the production units and the sales force. Some of it may contain only information, with the expectation that the production and/or sales units will adjust their activities so that they can tackle the developing situation. Frequently, specially when the change in the market situation is more pronounced, information in the downward communication is supported by instructions, which may range from suggestions to directives, on how to adjust to the new situation.

Upward Communication

Vertical communication upwards can be broadly divided into two kinds. First, there are routine reports of production or sales which are sent by the production or sales units at regular intervals. A company may have a system of monthly reports, another may want weekly reports. Those which have large-scale delegation of powers enabling production and sales units to chart their course without guidance may even have annual reports to the corporate office from the production and sales units. But this is rare, since the dynamism of the market is such that it changes much more frequently, and sometimes very drastically, than on an annual basis. But even if there is a system of annual, or half-yearly or quarterly, reports there is nothing to prevent the corporate office from asking for *ad hoc* reports to deal with a developing situation.

There is usually a set pattern and format of an upward communication giving business reports. This is explained in detail in a whole chapter where sample formats are given, so this need not detain us here.

One kind of routine reports are called production reports. When such a report comes from a manufacturing unit, it is understandable enough. But reports of sales units are also usually called production reports. This is because, in commercial terms, it is the production of value that counts. Value is produced not merely by manufacturing units but by sales organizations which book orders and thus produce value for the commercial enterprise.

Progress Report

Another kind of business report is the progress report, but this is not frequent in a protected, static market, now derisively called the command-and-control economy. The prime example of a command-and-control economy was the erstwhile Soviet Union. Now dissolved and broken up into its constituent republics which are independent and sovereign, the Soviet Union was an experiment in a centrally directed economy.

The Soviet Planning Commission–which was an innovation in any country's economic management–decided, through projections of the people's needs and demands, how much of a commodity the economy would need at a future date.

This having been decided, it was determined which centers could provide the most convenient and economical production facilities. The considerations were the availability of raw materials, the proximity and needs of the market and the climatic conditions. If, for instance, four locations had easy access to raw materials, they were chosen for the establishment of four production facilities. It was also decided which facility could most conveniently and economically feed which market.

If there was a production facility for a commodity in the Soviet Far East, a second in European Russia which is in the Far West, a third in a Central Asian republic and a fourth in the Caucasus, the produce of the facility in European Russia would not be available in the Far East, which would be fed by the facility located in that area.

In one way the arrangement made sense, since it would only add to the cost if goods produced in the Far West were transported to the Far East or the Central Asian region for consumption. Each consuming area would get goods produced in the facility located within it or nearest to it, reducing transportation cost. It would also reduce the burden on the transportation system.

Since all production facilities were state-owned, it would not make a difference either to the profitability of the facilities or to the consumer.

Rajaji's Caveat

In some cases, the price for the consumer was equalized all over the Soviet Union. If the Far West facility produced the commodity cheaper than the Far East facility and the consumer price was the same, the extra profit of one would offset the lower profit or loss of the other. Yet another advantage was that there would be no competitive advertising, saving money. The commodity would therefore be cheaper.

India to an extent emulated this model through what is called the licence-permit raj, a term coined in 1958 by the inimitable C Rajagopalachari, commonly called Rajaji. Licences or permits would be issued only for that level of production which the Indian Planning Commission projected as the demand at a particular future date.

The model looks fine except for two major drawbacks. First, it killed competition, which left the consumer at the mercy of the producer. Hence no production facility made an effort to lure consumers by offering attractive prices or incentives.

Dettol, to take a random example from today when the licence-permit raj has to an extent been ended, offers cakes of soap in two packages. You either buy a one-cake pack at a certain price or you buy a two-cake pack for less than the combined prices of two one-cake packs. The consumer who has liquidity or the one who issues two cakes simultaneously for different uses by the family can buy a two-cake pack and save money.

This did not happen under the Soviet system because producers of goods and services had no competition in their particular regions and therefore no incentive to think up the stratagem of a two-cake pack.

The second drawback was that no producer had an incentive to innovate or invent, having been given a fixed and protected market. The major and long-term loss was the drying up of the springs of innovation and enterprise. Another loss was that the market became static. It grew at a rate lower than it would if there were competition.

Nowadays we sometimes see two commodities selling together as one. A big carton of corn flakes may have a cake of soap coming ostensible free with it. What happens is that the corn flakes producer buys cakes of soap at wholesale rates, then adds the price he has paid for the soap to the price of the carton of corn flakes and fixes the sale price of the carton. For the consumer, the soap comes free of cost.

Two-in-one Strategy

Supposing the cost of production of a cake of soap is Rs. 5. Add 10% as the producer's profit, and it should be available to the consumer for Rs. 5.50. But marketing the soap as a separate commodity entails expenditure on cartage, insurance and the profit margin of stockists, sole selling agents and the retailer, and the price paid by the consumer swells to Rs. 10 or more. If, on the other hand, it sells combined with a big carton of corn flakes as a single commodity, the consumer gets the soap for Rs. 5.50 which the corn flakes maker paid to the soap producer. This way, consumption grows, so does production and so do employment and the economy.

Yet another drawback of a command-and-control or licence-permit economy is that if estimates of future demand go wrong, there is a shortage or overproduction with no quick remedy. For, all the initiative lies with the central planning authority. If supply from the Far East production facility falls short of demand, there can be black marketing, or the commodity may just not be available to the needy. There may be queues or even rationing with longer queues.

People who built houses before cement was freed of production and price controls would vouch how much they had to run around for it. I know because my house was built when the planners' calculation went wrong and the production of cement lagged behind demand.

Central Planners

A major characteristic of the command-and-control economy or the licence-permit raj is that most of the communication which makes the difference is downwards. The central planners, sitting in the capital, decide, on the basis of whatever data they have, whether and how to increase or reduce production and improve distribution. They also decide whether to expand production facilities and, if so, where and by how much.

Those actually producing or distributing the commodity in a particular region, and who therefore are on the spot and know intimately what is needed to be done, have no reason to make suggestions. There are wise men sitting in a central place and having a vision of the whole economy. They must decide. In fact alerting them about the changing situation may be construed as throwing one's weight about. So most of the upward communication tends to consist of routine reports which are mandatory.

In a tightly controlled one-party state like the erstwhile Soviet Union, some of the upward communication may even consist of praise for the wisdom of the central planners even if the situation on the ground is deteriorating. Most importantly, constructive suggestion on how to tackle an emerging situation dries up. Thus, in place of thousands of brains involved in the production and distribution of commodities, only one brain, or the set of brains involved in planning the production of commodities, would be exercised over the problem.

The rest of the brain power would be wasted. In fact, since the idle mind is the devil's workshop, a vast amount of brain power would most likely be used for such destructive purposes as how to trip the foreman or the plant manager.

Source of Growth

Upward communication, which means communication emanating from the ground level or from close to the ground, is a great source of sustenance and growth in a business organization functioning in a free market economy. Those who plan for the organization have a stream of data and suggestions about the ground situation fed free of cost by the production and sales force in particular areas.

In a command-and-control economy, such data come from field workers recruited to do the job for a salary. These workers may or may not be from the area they are posted in, and in any case the priority is to follow the prescribed procedure and fill up the prescribed forms.

Most importantly, the central planners face no threat of dissent or protest, since the data providers are content to collect and transmit the data and collect the salary. What Big Boss does with the data does not bother them. If the same job is done by the production and/or sales force based in the area, they would be more insistent that the data be put to good use. If this is not done, their own performance–production or sales–would suffer.

Most of the upward communication consists of hard ground level realities when made by those involved in production and sales. A sales force based in a given area will make heavy advance bookings if the demand is outstripping supply and insist that the orders be fulfilled in good time, otherwise the sales force loses face. If sales are slack, the bookings will be low, giving an indication to the planners that something is wrong – either the quality is not good enough or the consumers are finding alternative ways to fulfil their needs.

Another Channel

The more successful organizations keep yet another channel open for upward communication. They welcome suggestions both from consumers and staff and evaluate them very carefully for anything valuable. There are also complaint books.

But the acid test is how the suggestions or complaints are treated. In a command-and-control economy the central planner is mentally conditioned to think he knows best. For, wasn't he the chosen one to plan for the whole economy? The underlings are, after all, underlings. They would be planning, not he, if they knew better.

In a free market economy, in contrast, suggestions and complaints from consumers and junior staff are given great value. After all, they are the people on the spot. They feel and know the ground conditions from day to day.

A decade ago, I went from Delhi on a conducted tour of Garhwal organized by the Garhwal Mandal Vikas Nigam (Garhwal region development corporation), a Government organization. It was a package deal. The tourist paid a lump sum in advance. In exchange, he was taken by bus to various tourist destinations. On the way there were low-cost hotels and restaurants owned by the Nigam where the bus stopped for fixed periods. The tourists were expected to finish their eating and sightseeing within the time allotted. At night fell, they were parked for the overnight stay at Nigam-owned hotels where the rooms and dormitories were earmarked for them.

A Mis-conductor

I noticed that the conductor in charge of the tour invariably stopped the bus at breakfast, lunch and tea time not at the Nigam-owned restaurants, which were carefully positioned in a market area with many eateries, but at out of the way stopgap eating places where there were no other eateries.

On return I wrote the Nigam pointing this out. This meant loss of business to the Nigam-owned restaurants and inconvenience to the tourists who had to eat whatever was available at whatever price and of whatever quality, since there was no alternative.

There was no response. I wrote again. A month later the Nigam replied it would look into the matter and let me know. Two decades have passed and there has been no further communication. The Nigam boss in charge of the tourist trips apparently thinks he knows best. I have, naturally, never again gone on such a trip, though I have visited scenic Garhwal several times since to spend a week or so in the hills during the summer.

Some organizations take upward communication so seriously that they extend the complaints-and-suggestions formula to an "open house". If the "open house" is meant for employees, they are invited to air their views, including complaints and suggestions, at a convenient place and time and Big Boss listens and discusses and tries to find a way to improve things.

A similar exercise is gone through with customers. But this is productive only in a free market economy where the competitor is hot on the heels. If this exercise is gone through in a command-and-control situation, it is only a ritual.

Horizontal communication is that which takes place between individuals or groups of more or less equal rank. A worker operating a lathe machine may exchange notes about how it is going with another worker operating a lathe. Sometimes they learn from each other. When one operator finds his lathe giving trouble in a particular operation, his exchange of information with another operator may enable him to learn how the second operator has overcome the problem.

A group of volunteers removing garbage from one block of a colony may exchange notes with another group doing the same job in another block. They may tell each other how they encountered resistance from some residents, or how they persuaded them to cooperate in the completion of the task. This can be mutually beneficial. It can even generate healthy competition on which group completes the task first, or which block ends up the cleanest consequent on the labours of he group detailed to clean it.

Grapevine

Frequently, however, horizontal communication degenerates into gossip or, what is worse, hearsay. People working in adjoining units often exchange notes with each other on what they have heard others say. In one case there was a short circuit in a corner of a big factory. The resulting fire was put out quickly, but not before the dozen or so people working in that corner had to evacuate it as a precaution.

People in adjoining units saw or heard of it. One person told another and in time workers in a far end of the factory got alarmed that a huge fire had broken out. It required a huge PR exercise and spot visits by delegations of workers from distant units to prevent it from snowballing.

All of us have read in newspaper reports of the "grapevine" divulging some secret or the other, usually alarming, to a reporter or a few reporters.

All the reporters of course find out the official version, but they also make informal inquiries. For, no reporter worth his salt will depend solely on what is officially stated. There can be other versions which can be at variance with the official version. It is here that the grapevine comes in. The perceptive reporter is able to separate grain from chaff, eye-witness and informed accounts from hearsay, and reports only that which bears credibility.

One example of reporting from the grapevine is the spin made of the exclusion of Anil Kumble from a Test match during the 2002 cricket tour of the West Indies. A number of Indian reporters (though not all) touring with the team quoted the grapevine to the effect that this was skipper Saurav Ganguly's revenge for his exclusion from the playing eleven of a Test during an earlier tour of the West Indies when Kumble was the vice-captain.

Saurav told a reporter who had refrained from quoting the grapevine he didn't even recall having been excluded from the playing eleven when Kumble was the vice-captain. "Tell me," he added, "how do you fit two spinners into the team on a wicket which does not suit spin bowling?"

SUMMING UP

Communication in a business organization can be vertical or horizontal. Vertical communication can be downwards or upwards. Downward communication can be an order, instruction, information or advice from a boss to his subordinate colleagues. It is upwards when the subordinate colleague (or colleagues) reports what he has done and the results of this action to the boss.

Downward communication can be *chain* or *cluster*. Chain communication takes place when the boss gives an order to a sub-boss or a number of sub-bosses to pass on down to line to subordinate colleagues and to ensure implementation. Cluster is when the same communication is addressed to more than one sub-boss. A typical example is the circular.

In a command-and-control economy, downward communication dominates and shapes the course of development. In a free market economy, upward communication has as great a role to play as downward communication, since it gives feedback, which affects the course of development.

Self-Check Exercises

1. Explain two kinds of vertical communication.

   (Space for answer)

2. What is cluster communication? Give an example.

   (Space for answer)

3

Process of Communication: The Role of Encoding

Communication, a smile or a frown, oral or written, vertical or horizontal, upward or downward, begins with the communicator. Someone or a group decides that he has a message to convey to someone else or some other group.

General Ziaul Haq decided that he would not allow Jammu and Kashmir to remain part of the Indian Union. So when American and Chinese weapons and Saudi funding became available to raise on Pakistan territory an army to topple the Soviet-supported Government in Afghanistan, he recruited, trained and armed young men who were willing to make sacrifices to achieve his objective.

Earlier he had decided that the easiest way was to create an insurgency in Punjab based on Sikh discontent, real or imagined. This way the land link between Jammu and Kashmir and the rest of India could be cut, and the state would fall in Pakistan's lap like a ripe mango.

Ziaul Haq never said it in so many words. The message was conveyed coded in his actions, which consisted of harbouring, financing, training, and arming Sikh malcontents for sabotage and killing. India received the message, identified its transmitter and proceeded to crush the insurgency in Punjab.

The response, or feedback, was that India would not allow what Pakistan, through Ziaul Haq's plan, sought to achieve. It was coded in the form of the sustained campaign to crush the Punjab insurgency.

Patel's Coded Response

In the case cited in a previous chapter, the prince's message was that he would nor accede to the Indian Union. The code was that his ancestors had earned the right to rule in perpetuity. Sardar Patel decoded the message. His response was "no" to the prince's message. It was coded in silence. The prince decoded Patel's message as a rejection of his stand, so he went and signed the instrument of accession

This can be graphically depicted as follows:

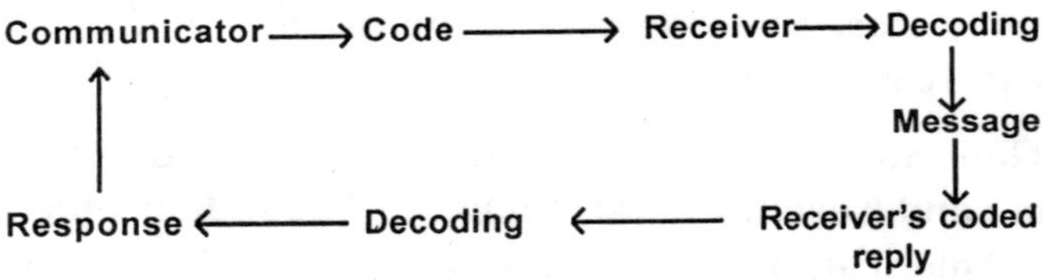

This is but one example of coding and decoding. Life is full of coded messages and responses, though there are plenty of messages which are barely coded. Consider the following:

Servant: It's 5 p.m. and work is finished.

Master: Bring a litre of milk from the dairy.

The servant's message is that he is going home. It is coded and said as above. The master's message in response, as decoded, is "no". He indicates that the work is not yet finished by telling him to do something more. Even that may not "finish" the work since the milk may have to be boiled or tea made from it, but the master does not say so yet. That will be decided after the servant has brought the milk.

Volumes have been written about the virtues of direct communication. One of the expressions commonly used is to "call a spade a spade". Another is not to "beat about the bush". Many think the world would be a better place to live in if everyone called a spade a spade. Or if people did not beat about the bush.

Forgetfulness

But most of the people who have succeeded most markedly in the world frequently don't call a spade a spade. Jagjivan Ram, a high ranking member of Mrs. Gandhi's Cabinet, was in the late 1960s found to have not filed his income-tax return for three or four years running. Some young M.P.'s found this out and put a question in Parliament. Mrs. Gandhi, replying to the question, instead of calling a spade a spade, remarked: "Babuji (Mr. Jagjivan Ram) was guilty of some such forgetfulness."

Sir Winston Churchill faced a similar predicament when one of his Cabinet ministers was alleged by a member of the House of Commons to have given wrong information to Parliament. He rose up and phrased his reply thus: "There was a terminological inexactitude in his reply."

There are two schools of thought on this. One view, as noted earlier, is that if everyone was brutally frank and didn't beat about the bush, things would be much better. This, even if frankness caused embarrassment, even resentment, momentarily. The rival point of view is that if one's point can be made without causing bruises or hurt egos, that is preferable and profitable.

How Mathur Phrased It

When I joined the *Statesman* in 1964, I was given a lot of work and was under constant watch. From Day One, the composing room found it difficult to decipher my handwriting. Three days later a delegation led by the Foreman came to represent to Senior Chief Sub B D Mathur.

He listened with great attention, then took several hours charting his course. Having done so, he called me, asked me about my family and whether I found it uncomfortable living in a strange city without it. Then, with a diffident smile, he remarked, “The composing room finds your handwriting only slightly less bad than mine!” (The fact is, I learnt later, that it had found my handwriting indecipherable!).

Moved more by the tact with which Mathur had conveyed the composing room’s complaint, and the humility with which it had been conveyed to me, I took to spending precious time typing things out whenever my handwriting threatened to become illegible.

Mathur later told me he thought it would be foolish and counterproductive to condemn me outright, risking losing me. After all, I had been selected after a long search during which 34 other men had been tested and found wanting by News Editor C S Smith, an Australian whose judgment of men and their professional capabilities was held in high esteem.

Alexander’s Example

Alexander was the greatest conqueror of his time but he was known never to confront head on. In the battle with Porus, instead of directly engaging the enemy who was camped with a large army across the Jhelum, he moved a strong contingent of his troops several miles upstream to cross the river and attack Porus from the rear. After the battle, in which Porus was taken prisoner, Alexander asked him what kind of treatment he should be given. When Porus replied that he expected the treatment that a vanquished king received, Alexander stretched his hand of friendship. He got an enduring friend.

In contrast, further in the rear, when the vanquished had poured venom on him, Alexander had annexed his territory and appointed his general, Seleucos, to be the Governor of the conquered territory.

Even today, Pakistan is known to be the biggest sponsor of terrorists in the world and harbours, trains, arms and funds them for use in all kinds of places including Kashmir, but President George W Bush has studiously refrained from calling a spade a spade. Instead he keeps harping on "working with" Pakistan and General Musharraf to deal with the problem. This way he has managed to wean away from Afganistan's Taliban their biggest friend and supporter, turned it into an ally and uses its territory and forces to hunt for fleeing Taliban and Al Qaida fighters.

Cipher Communication

Coding a message may sound simple but depends heavily on who the receiver of the message is. It also depends on what the communicator wants to achieve.

Government communication with missions aboard, or with military units or concerning the deployment of security forces, is considered confidential. There are standard cipher codes and norms which are routinely used. These are known to those at the receiving end, who then proceed to decode it so that the message intended is correctly conveyed to those who are to use it.

If there is a suspicion that the cipher code is broken by those who should not know of the message, it is changed by those whose job it is to devise ever new codes to deal with such situations.

This is a mechanical work that goes on impersonally and routinely. In fact, most Governments maintain separate departments to devise new codes and to break the codes of other Governments.

During World War II, the British were able to break the German code and were therefore able to decipher most of the instructions sent by the German High Command to lower level formations fighting on the front.

At the non-Governmental level, encoding and decoding depend upon the audience addressed. I know of a couple whose firstborn craved incessantly for ice cream. It so happened that they lived in a house on the main road in the crowded market area of Karol Bagh in Delhi. Every few minutes there would pass in front of the house a push cart with the vendor crying *i-i-c-e c-r-e-a-m*, and the boy would pester his parents to buy enchanting stuff for him.

Coding for a Child

Apart from being heavy on the purse and a day-long irritant, it was bad for the child's health. Every week or 10 days he would be down with cold, cough and fever, and the culprit seemed to be the frequent eating of ice cream sold by street vendors from their push carts.

So, on the next weekly shopping day, the couple took the young one to a restaurant famous for its ice cream and *kulfi* and let the young one gorge on the stuff. They then told him this was hygienically prepared and won't cause sore throat and fever. The street vendor's *i-i-c-e c-r-e-a-m* in contrast was unclean and caused his weekly bouts of fever and sore throat.

The catch phrase they used to convince the five-year-old was that "*i-i-c-e c-r-e-a-m* brings sore throat and fever, ice cream is healthy."

From that day, the boy always clarified after every request that he was asking for ice cream and not *i-i-c-e c-r-e-a-m*.

Spelling It Out

Daily life is full of such innovations. A couple well versed in Urdu routinely spelled out loudly key words or sentences in Urdu if they did not want their two tiny tots to know what was being said. The catch was that the two children, both born after independence in 1947, were all at sea with Urdu spellings though they knew the words well enough.

An American story concerns a millionaire's son who was admitted to Harvard and devised a way to extract money from his tight-fisted father. Every time he scored high grades, he would spin out a yarn about how he had been dragged out by friends to an expensive restaurant to celebrate.

The wealthy man was particular that he should not be made to squander his hard-earned money. But he was even more keen that nobody should accuse him of keeping his son in penury. So he would meekly shell out the extra money that his son said had been spent on celebrations.

All that the son had to do was to craft his account of the event in such a way that it appeared he went broke every time he scored high grades.

SUMMING UP

Communication starts with the communicator. He is the one who decides that a communication has to be made. He decides on the message to be communicated, the party or person to be addressed and the channel of communication.

He then proceeds to encode the message and transmits it. The receiver receives the coded message, decodes it, and responds.

Response is also called feedback. It is also encoded and transmitted back to the original communicator, who decodes it and gets the message.

Self-Check Exercises

1. Write three paragraphs explaining the process of communication.

   (Space for answer)

2. Give an example from your experience of coded communication.

   (Space for answer)

4

The Art of Listening and Decoding

The message, direct or coded, is but one part of the communication process. On one side of it is the transmitter who designs, encodes and transmits it, on the other is the receiver. Communication takes place only when it is received, decoded and a response is given, again direct or coded, verbally or non-verbally.

Receiving and decoding a message also requires skill. If the message is oral, it should be listened to, decoded and analyzed carefully. Let us look at a bland statement:

When I return, we will plan how to solve the problem.

The listener can go to sleep thinking he has free time until his friend returns. Right? Wrong. The following messages are coded in this sentence:

1. The planning will take place when the friend returns.
2. Ways to solve the problem will be devised.
3. The two will do the devising, since "we" includes both.
4. The listener should, therefore, be available and ready when the friend returns.

The smart listener will turn the problem over in his mind and think of ways to solve it. For, "we" implies that he is expected to make a contribution. He is also to wait, while he thinks, for his friend's return and not to go away or to be found sleeping.

Athelstane the Unready

Sir Walter Scott's novel *lvanhoe* has a knight named Athelstane who is a cosummate fighter capable of worsting in combat the most skilful of warriors. But Scott calls him "Athelstane the Unready" since he took time to respond. Unlike Athelstane, our recipient of the message should be ready, his plan of action well thought out, when the friend returns.

Good listening involves finding an area of interest with the transmitter in which one can contribute, judging the content of the message including the style of delivery, suspending one's verdict until the message has been delivered and absorbed. The listener has to look for ideas in the message, making listening an active and not a passive exercise. One has to resist distractions which may make him miss the whole or part of the message and keep the mind open for ideas instead of sticking to preconceived notions.

Bad listening is characterized by condemning the subject being covered as uninteresting, or being critical of the transmitter's style of delivery, because if one does so one is likely to miss the content, evading the difficult or technical portions or succumbing to emotion which may, again, make one miss the content.

Of the hurdles to good listening, distractions are one of the most innocent looking but one of the most difficult to cross. Everyone will think of the child crying, the pressure cooker whistle going off, or a visitor knocking on the door as the most distracting. But these are only external distractions which are considered by psychologists as peripheral.

There are distractions in the mind which are more formidable. Many people let their mind wander, thinking that listening is a passive exercise. It is not. Active involvement is necessary. The biggest culprit is planning for the future while listening. Many think they have understood the message when they have heard part of it and start formulating their response. They are liable to miss an operative part of the message.

Full-time Job

At school all of us learnt a poem starting with "One thing at a time, and that done well". The fact is that listening is a full-time job. Indeed one should decide in advance whether the message is worth listening to. If it is, it is worth giving full attention to.

When listening to a lecture, it is important to know how to take notes. It is almost suicidal to take down all or most of what is said, for one cannot listen and write at the same time. Each requires full attention. The trick is to note catch-words or catch-phrases and listen to the rest with rapt attention. For this one has to train himself, and this is not difficult. All successful journalists do it, and that is how they are able to report whole speeches.

To give an example, if it is about Pokharan I, which was India's first nuclear test carried out in 1974, one can take down the catch-phrase *The Buddha Is Smiling*. If one has listened carefully, this catch-phrase will bring to the mind all that was said about the preparation for and all that went on during the test. The magic that the catch-word or catch-phrase can work has been explained in detail in the chapter *How To Get News; The Journalist's Secret* in my book *12 ½ Management Mantras of Journalism*.

Things to Notice

While listening one has to notice, apart from the words, the tone and pitch of the voice, facial expressions, gestures and posture and, apart from all this, what is left unsaid. A study by the reputed NGO Consumer Unity and Trust Society

(CUTS), Jaipur, shows that "when conversing, less than one-third of the communication is verbal, with more than 65 per cent of the social meaning being conveyed by silent speech signals. This means that during a typical exchange more than half the messages received and sent will be visual rather than verbal." (*Reaching Out: A Training Manual for Skills in Communication*).

Have you noticed that in criminal cases, especially when a man has died, eye-witness accounts usually prove decisive? What is heard is never so decisive, and is frequently termed as hearsay and not admitted in evidence. An eye-witness account can only be made suspect by another eye-witness account if the second one is equally convincing. Aural evidence, that is, what one heard, can never override an eye-witness account.

Eye-witness vs. Hearsay

A man testifying that he saw the accused behead the victim with an axe will be decisive in a murder case for conviction. If the accused's witnesses testify that they heard that the accused was in a town 500 miles away, it can never over-ride an eye-witness account of the killing. But if a witness testifies that he saw and met the accused on the day and at the time of the killing 500 miles away, the eye-witness account of the killing will become suspect and subject to further verification and investigation.

Similarly, a man's evidence that he heard shooting accompanied by the victim's cry that "John has shot me" will carry less weight than evidence by another man that he met John at a wedding 500 miles away on the day and at the time of the shooting.

Non-judicial Example

Non-judicial experience corroborates this. I can recall the faces and bearings of my teachers over the 16 years that

I attended school and college and can even draw the sketches of all of them. And this, mind you, though the last time I attended any class was 42 years ago! But I can recall only snatches of what they said, and not the exact words.

Try this test. You met a man an hour ago. You recall what he looked like, the clothes he wore and whether he wore glasses and had a beard, even if you met him only for five minutes. He spoke five sentences within your hearing in those five minutes. Can you recall what he said? More importantly, can you recall the exact words in which he framed his sentences? Try to recall which of the following sentences he uttered:

I will come if invited.

I can come if invited.

I will consider coming.

I may come if an invitation is extended.

Let them invite me, and I'm there.

An invitation is necessary before I come.

An invitation is necessary before I consider it.

The reason is that seeing creates an image on the brain. Hearing only gives a sensation of change, there is no image, exact or inexact. When you hear a sentence, by reflex action you decode it and absorb only the decoded message, not the exact words.

The Threat

When a man says "there will be dire consequences if he is even seen near my fiancée's house", what the brain records is the threat. The man may be killed if he is seen near the girl's house, or kidnapped, or may have to bear some other form of reprisal like the burning of his house, an attack on his parents or only an FIR to the police.

The exact impression will depend upon what image you have of the man in your mind. On the other hand, if you have seen a man attack the victim with an axe, the earlier mental image of the attacker you had–that he is the non-violent type, timid or effeminate–will be overhauled.

Eye and Ear

Science tells us that whereas sound waves travel at a speed of 100 ft per second at sea level, light waves travel at 186,000 miles per second. The human ear is sensitive to sound frequencies of 50 to 15000 per second (hence ultrasound tests by doctors using sound vibrations which the human ear cannot detect). The eye can detect light at 10,000,000,000,000,000 cycles per second.

So the brain starts recording visual images of the man you meet long, long before it notices any sound that he makes and continues to record visual images long after he has ceased to make any sound. Hence, observation of a man, his gestures, his clothes and how he carries himself have the potential to tell you much apart from what he articulates in words. Besides, he may speak nothing, but he cannot prevent you from observing him.

A common pastime in schools and colleges is to line up the whole class and whisper a sentence to one member. He whispers what he has heard to his neighbour, who in turn whispers to his own neighbour. When the message reaches the last boy or girl, it may be very different from the original sentence. If the sentence was "a tall, muscular man with moustaches wants to see you", it may end up as "beware, the devil is after you".

Coca-Cola Case

This is not saying that what you see is necessarily conclusive and overrides what you hear. In a recent case, a court restrained Coca-Cola from airing a television advertisement which is derisive of a tall man bearded like Amitabh Bachchan and his short thickset companion who are flying kites. The complaint to the court was that it lambasted Bachchan and his short companion, Sachin Tendulkar, both of whom are idolized by people and who had appeared in an earlier Pepsi advertisement flying kites in a similar fashion.

Coca-Cola could argue that the advertisement only showed a tall and bearded man and a short thickset man flying kites. No word was said that they were Amitabh and Sachin. If Coca-Cola had made this contention, it would merit serious consideration in appeal, since what is seen need not be what it looks like.

The lesson in communication is that neither the spoken word nor appearance is final and incontrovertible. What is decisive is the total effect. Listening includes visual observation, and decoding must take both into account if one is to correctly understand what the other person is saying.

SUMMING UP

Listening is a job requiring full attention. It includes deciphering (or decoding) body language and gestures, and the tone and pitch of oral communication. Usually it includes all of these functions.

An encoded communication can convey more than one message. When a person, instead of replying directly to a servant's question whether he can go home, asks him to prepare tea for five guests, the coded message is that it is not yet time to go home. Further, if tea is being prepared for guests, it may have to be served. The third message is that it will be time only after tea has been prepared and possibly served, that it will be decided whether it is time to go home.

Self-Check Exercises

1. Write two sentences each about three kinds of distractions to listening.

   (Space for answer)

2. What are catch-words? How do they help in getting the messages of a speaker at a public meeting?

   (Space for answer)

Your Attention, Please!

John Maynard Keynes, famous for the Keynsian theory in economics, once called on President Roosevelt. Through his New Deal, Roosevelt had pulled America out of the Great Depression of the 1930s largely by using methods conceptualized and advocated by Keynes. This had spurred construction, consumption, production, growth and employment.

Keynes possibly wanted to know from the horse's mouth what his experience of using Keynesian tools was and to thank him. Or, possibly, he wanted to know if the American President had any new ideas based on his experience. He started the discussion, but he had barely started when the telephone rang.

When Roosevelt had finished his telephone conversation, Keynes started again. Again the telephone rang and again Roosevelt picked it up. The conversation interrupted a second time, Keynes held his peace. When it ended, he started again.

When the conversation was interrupted once again by the telephone, Keynes made up his mind. He excused himself and left.

After some time, Keynes telephoned. When Roosevelt expressed surprise why he had left without a discussion, Keynes replied: "I realize that the telephone is the only way to get your attention."

5

Time Management and Fixing Priorities

Management can be of oneself or of others. Management of oneself is a matter of one's personal journey through life. What we are studying in this chapter is the management of others. Right?

Wrong, since no one makes the journey of life all by himself. Every man is a member of society. Even if he chooses to remain single, everyone must have a father and a mother. The majority have siblings, and through siblings they get into other relationships – siblings' spouses and their families, siblings' children and their friends, sweethearts, neighbours, other community members, clubs, religious groups, linguistic groups, etc.

Worth Befriending

Cartoonist Bireshwar of the *National Herald* of Lucknow proudly proclaimed all the five years we worked together in the 1960s that he was particular to keep his distance from people. He came to work early, visualized his daily cartoon idea, discussed and finalized it with the Editor, crafted the cartoon, returned home, ate his dinner and went to bed.

Two decades later I went to Lucknow from Delhi and, having time on my hands, went to Bireshwar's house to find out how he was doing. I had always thought he was a simple man whom I considered to be worth befriending even though he insisted on keeping his distance.

"Fine," he said in one word, as was his wont. Any more cartoons? "Not one since I retired," he replied matter-of-factly, adding, "You know I like to live by myself."

Even as I was wondering how to keep the conversation going, he excused himself. He had to attend a *pravachan* by his guru that started in five minutes' time!

24 Hours

The fact is that everyone has 24 hours on his hands. It may seem too little to some, but for others it may not be easy to traverse all alone. In this time each one has to go through his daily ablutions, eat and clean, rest, exercise and do other things to keep mind and body healthy. He must interact constantly with society and has to manage many things, situations and people.

If a chair is broken, he can go to the carpenter only within a particular time frame. He cannot go knocking at the carpenter's door at midnight since it is the time for the carpenter to rest. He can go only when the carpenter is at his workshop.

Further, for a repair job no carpenter struggling to supply an order worth lakhs of rupees is going to be bothered. So he must find a carpenter who takes on such puny jobs.

Bireshwar's guru could not be bothered to wait for just one of his disciples to arrive before starting his *pravachan*. The disciple had learnt through life that he, like others, had to manage his 24 hours in a way as to do all that he needed to do within the time he had.

Yet he believed, no doubt in all sincerity, that he lived by himself and had the barest need for others.

The fact is that time management is an essential part of life, as much for reluctant as for enthusiastic members of society. It equally affects everyone, as much individuals as managers, for in both capacities everyone has but 24 hours at his disposal. Like the rays of the sun, it permeates all layers of life even if many do not realize it.

There are several less realized ramifications of this. Everyone knows that smokers tend to die earlier than non-smokers. We also know that ailments connected with or resulting from smoking take up more of the time and energy of smokers than of non-smokers. A Norwegian study covering 50,000 people, published by the *New England Journal of Medicine*, has now found that those who smoke find it less easy to manage their tasks within a given time frame than non-smokers, other things remaining the same.

Fitness Test

Another misconception is that keeping fit is for athletes. Others can relax. In this cricket-mad country one reads every other day in newspapers that some player or the other will have to undergo a fitness test before being cleared for a match. Has anyone ever read a news item saying that a manager will have to undergo a fitness test before he is allowed to run a factory? Or that a housewife will have to pass a fitness test before being allowed to do housework?

Yet, fitness is as necessary for a factory manage to deliver goods on time and for the housewife to prepare the child for school as for Sachin Tendulkar to score a century in a Test match.

Americans are great at quantifying efficiency in work and management. The Center for Creative Leadership (CCL) at Colorado Springs, Colorado, collected data all through the 1990s from the thousands who attended its many seminars. It was found that those who exercised regularly performed their jobs much better than those who did not. The inference drawn was that regular exercise enables one to mobilize his energy faster and in a more focused form.

The irony was that those who routinely skipped exercise blamed "lack of time" and "conflict with work" for this, yet they spent less time at work on the average than those who religiously exercised mind and body.

Prioritization

The second key factor that makes the difference between good, routine, mediocre and rank bad management is what priority one gives to which task. Each one of us starts the day with a list of things to do. The more meticulous ones among us write out the list, but most of us trust the memory.

It is not uncommon to hear some people exclaim at the end of the day, "I couldn't find time" for some key task, or "Sorry, I clean forgot about it." The culprit really is not lack of time but faulty prioritization.

Many go through life like a clock, ticking two after one, three after two. There is no prioritization for them. Life goes on today as it went off yesterday, and will go on tomorrow as it went off today. Ablutions, washing, eating, dressing, going to work, returning home, eating, hitting the bed...... In the process the agenda – which job must necessarily be executed, which next, and which if there is time – gets turned topsy turvy.

I once received a police notice for a minor violation of a traffic rule. It was such a minor matter that I decided to drive to the magistrate's chamber at 11 a.m. on the appointed day, pay the fine and be done with it. But reaching my Institute at nine I plunged into the research project in hand. Only on receiving a call from home whether I was at the magistrate's chamber did I rush there to pay the fine.

The mind was too full of the research project, and in the day's priorities I had neglected to mark the attendance before the magistrate. The negligence could have amounted to contempt, earning penal action.

How to List Priorities

The key is how one lists his day's agenda. Certain routine things like eating, dressing, etc., need not even be listed. They are done as a habit or by reflex action. Yet, if one sits down to list the day's tasks, routine things tend to come first to the mind. The crucial non-routine task will tend to be relegated to the 20th or 25th place, whereas it is this task that should get top priority. One can live without eating for a day, but omitting to attend court on the appointed day will earn you a penalty.

The supply of every input man needs to go through life is limited whereas demand is unlimited. This applies to all his material and non-material needs, including time. Hence, time management is as important as management of money. The person who manages his time better can put in a lot more of work, accounting for better and greater output in quality and quantity than one who is a bad time manager.

Similarly about prioritization. The man who does a lot of low priority work and neglects a crucial task may look more busy. But the one who has his priorities right will be more productive and successful.

SUMMING UP

Everyone is part of society, reluctant or willing. No one can go through life all by himself.

The day consists of 24 hours for everyone, but every task man undertakes demands time. Hence the person who manages his time better can get through a lot more of work of better quality than one who is a poor time manager.

Good time management can be accomplished by listing the tasks one has to perform in order of priority. The tasks that necessarily must be done during the day must get top priority. Less important tasks should be listed lower down until one reaches the tasks that can be left undone if time runs out.

Self-Check Exercises

1. Write in three sentences what is meant by time management.

   (Space for answer)

2. Why is prioritization crucial?

   (Space for answer)

6

Image-Building and the Making of a Brand

Every business organization, indeed every business man and every business manager, has an image. After an image has been created, it has to be maintained and improved. The image JRD Tata had was of a trustworthy, go-getting and visionary business man. It was created by him. It was not inherited, except that one hoped that the scion of an illustrious business family would be capable of maintaining the business.

If he had, by the time he was the grand old man of Indian business, an image of a man who turned everything he touched into gold, it was entirely his own creation.

After World War II, the American Government decided that the fleet of Dakota transport planes it had built up in India would be best disposed of locally. Ferrying them back to the USA would be costly, and even if they were flown back they would not be able to stand competition from the brand new improved models which were swarming the American skies.

A large number of Indian business houses which had made piles of money during the war bought and refurbished the Dakotas and started airlines. The Tata house was one of them.

Karachi to Bombay

JRD Tata had a passion for flying. Two decades earlier he had become the first Indian to become a pilot. He flew the first civilian Indian flight, a tiny Tiger Moth plane, from Karachi to Bombay. Now that there was an opportunity, he founded the Tata Airlines.

To begin with, Tata's airline was one of the many, all of which flew Dakotas. But while most of the others concentrated on milking the new opportunity, Tata had a vision for the future. He created a benchmark for punctuality, courtesy, comfort and safety. He also visualized expansion by the acquisition of newer, more efficient, more sophisticated and larger aircraft.

This was his image when the Government of India decided to create a national airline. JRD Tata was the man selected to run it.

The Situation in 1945

Now, in 2006, when the Government is moving out of business and the *mantra* is to shed the government holding to the highest bidder, it is difficult to visualize the situation half a century ago when the Government invested money and handed over the enterprises to a private citizen or business house to run. But this is what happened in the case of civil aviation when all the private airlines were taken over to form Air-India International, which was then handed over to JRD Tata to run.

Why this was a momentous decision will be clear when we realize the atmosphere that prevailed 60 years ago.

During the six years of the war (1939-45) everything, from foodgrains to consumer goods, became scarce as all resources were devoted to the prosecution of the war. Imports were restricted. Prices galloped, but incomes stagnated. There was widespread suspicion that traders and business men had hoarded goods to reap windfall profits. Business men as a class had come to be regarded as bloodsuckers.

Why JRD Tata ?

It was in this atmosphere that JRD Tata was handpicked by Jawaharlal Nehru to run the national airline. He was chosen for his clean, honest, forward-looking image. In whatever he had done, he had shown vision for the future of society as distinct from the vision for himself and his business house.

Air-India prospered and became one of the favourite airlines of travelers across the world. It was noted for its punctuality, efficiency, courtesy, comfort, safety and reliability. This was unbelievable for the world, yet it was a fact. Unbelievable since, let us remember, India was the only officially slave country in the world until 1947.

Most of Asia and Africa were under the tutelage of various European powers. But they were all colonies or protectorates, *de jure* or *de facto*. Britain controlled dozens of territories across the world, but the King was the Emperor only of India, not of, for instance, Nigeria, Rhodesia or Guyana.

For such a country to run an international airline on equal terms with the USA, Britain, France and other advanced countries was a feat unprecedented in the world. Not only this, JRD Tata was known not to have sought or obtained any advantage or profit for himself or for the house of Tatas from the situation. That is what made him a legend in his lifetime. Tata became a brand.

Other Enterprises

Air-India's success, however, made many a man who wielded power salivate with greed. Even as Air-India was created and thrived, dozens of other Government enterprises were started. Inevitably, those who made the plans came to

J.R.D. Tata enjoying the foray into civil aviation as visualised by cartoonist Dhir.
Courtesy: The Hit Parade

head them. ICS (later IAS) officers, politicians and others ran these enterprises with we now know what results.

The state Governments, with their bigger quota of officers and politicians, next stepped in, starting commercial enterprises at the taxpayer's expense. Finally came the situation when those who ran these enterprises thought, "If we can run these enterprises, why not Air-India?"

Now that disinvestment is on the anvil, those who have profited at Air-India's expense are fighting a rearguard action to prevent what they derisively call privatization and which they equate with selling the family silver.

This short account of the rise and decline of Air-India is necessary if we are to realize how inextricably the prospects of a business enterprise are linked with the image of the business house or business man who has built it up and nurtured it. For, image is created not by taking out full page advertisements in newspapers. It is created by such basic qualities as honesty, persistence, vision and daring.

Public Relations

Image-building came to be recognized as an exercise worth doing early in the 20th century. An American coined the expression public relations. It consists of showing to the world the positive qualities which we have and which we can utilize for the common good.

The qualities which the world values are trustworthiness, sticking to time in the execution of projects, and excellence in the quality of production. If these qualities are assured, the world will be willing to give a higher reward for them, whereas where quality is suspect and the word of the producer cannot be trusted, the reward will be given grudgingly and in a smaller measure.

This has led to the rise of the awareness of brands. Business enterprises, or even individual business men, now try to create brand awareness. Brand awareness means that the user of a brand of products feels assured that the service will be on time, trustworthy, of good quality and reliable.

Two Phenomena

This has led to two phenomena of which every consumer or user of a product must be aware. *First*, goods of a particular brand are able to demand and obtain relatively higher prices. For, the awareness is spreading that quality and trustworthiness have to come at a price since ensuring these entails extra cost.

Until a few years ago, when Usha sewing machines were very popular and a number of enterprises grew up to cash in on the phenomenon by offering cheaper substitutes, the Usha punch line which worked ran *ghar ghar mein silai, Usha ne chalai* (Usha made sewing popular as a household activity).

Here is another example which illustrates the *second* phenomenon. The Tata brand has come to mean quality, whether it is Tata tea, Tata chemicals, Tata steel or Tata automobiles. The Tata Institute of Fundamental Research was the womb from which the nation's atomic energy programme was born. No wonder, the stock advertisement of the Tata Iron and Steel Company (TISCO) lists things that the company does as social welfare projects, and then says, almost as an afterthought, "We also make steel." The message is that whatever the Tatas do, they do it excellently. That is the brand.

Tata Advertisement

The most recent Tata advertisement (reproduced here) does not talk of even one of the hundreds of products that the dozens of Tata companies make. It only talks of *Building India*, for which it has launched all-India essay competitions for school children.

Even the prizes promised are not products of any Tata

The Building India Advertisement

company. They are high-tech gizmos costing thousands of rupees each produced by other companies.

The essay competitions are in three sections – 6th to 8th standards, 9th and 10th standards, and 11th and 12th standards. The competitions are running in six cities- Chennai, Bangalore, Kolkata, Mumbai, Hyderabad and Delhi. There are students from 40 selected schools participarting.

The Idea : *Build India*

The idea is to invite the youth of the country to join the Tata endeavour to *Build India*. Unlike product advertisements, this advertisement does not invite participants to buy a Tata product, or to write a slogan eulogizing a Tata-made product.

Nor is it a talent-spotting expedition. There is no obligation on any of the participants to join a Tata company. The only hope – not a condition but only a hope – is that the kids who take part in the competitions, plus also those who just stand and wait, will be inspired enough to join the great endeavour to *Build India.*

How they do it is left to them to decide. They may join a Tata enterprise, or they may not. They may embark on entrepreneurship or serve a company or the Government. The hope is that in whatever they do they will promote the goal of *Building India.*

This is the message of the brand. How many other brands have sent out such a message?

Brand Awareness

Enormous as JRD Tata's contribution was to brand-building, the man who created brand awareness in India was patriarch Sir Jamsetji N. Tata (1839-1904).

At a time when even pins and needles were imported from Sheffield, he envisioned the mother of all steel products. In what was then a wilderness in Jharkhand, he created an integrated steel plant in and around the backward village of Sakchi. Not only that, he proceeded to clear the thick brush to found a township.

In time this township developed into Jameshedpur, the complete steel city with all civic services provided by the Tatas. Sir Jamsetji successor, Dorabji, and then most crucially JRD Tata's huge contribution was to convert this dream into the very well diversified brand Tata.

And not merely a huge commercial brand. The Tata companies have together developed into the largest collective philanthropic brand in the country. The country's best hospitals, the best and largest institutions of higher learning, and institutions carrying out the most cutting edge research are founded by the Tatas.

Not many know that Tata Sons Ltd., the holding company, hardly distributes any dividends. There are two channels in which the earnings of Tata Sons Ltd. flow.

One is to build up the brand, which includes the Tata brand and now also the *Build India brand*.

The Other Channel

The other channel is charity. All the many Tata institutions – like the Tata Institute of Fundamental Research, the Tata Memorial Hospital and the Tata Institute of Social Science Research – have a built-in provision in the earnings of Tata Sons Ltd. for their unkeep. The Board of Directors does not have to appropriate particular sums for these institutions. These sums go to the institutions as a matter of course.

And not only unkeep. Their further development is also provided for automatically. Like the Tata brand commercial products, the Tata charitable institutions also continuously strive to be the very best in India. In fact, these institutions have themselves developed into a much-envied and much-emulated brand of philanthropy.

Yet JRD Tata had no magic wand. His trump card was continued and continuing attention to the details of whatever institutions he established or supported.

R M Lala, who has written a very perceptive biography of the great man, recounts how no detail escaped his attention if it helped upgrade quality at a Tata company or philanthropic institution.

Those days (as now), it was customary for women to wear "matching colors." For instance, the lipstick had to be the same colour as the sari.

On one flight, JRD Tata found Air-India's air hostesses wearing white lipstick to go with their customised white silk saris. He was all politeness to the hostesses, but wrote to the Personnel Director that the white lipstick with white silk saris made the beautiful girls look like corpses wrapped in white.

Promptly, lipstick that suited the girls' complexion and personality replaced the white.

The Human Side

Yet, JRD Tata was not a mere workaholic driving the employees relentlessly. He was intensely human, with a great sense of humour. He was on first name terms will all employees. They called him Jeh, short for Jehangir which was his first name.

The story is told that once somebody wrote a letter to him with the salutation "Dear Jay..". The big man promptly wrote back : "I have looked up the dictionary and find that Jay is a 'noisy, chattering European bird with brilliant plumage' and, figuratively, 'an impertinent chatterer or simpleton.' For future reference, my name is spelt as Jeh, an abbreviation of Jehangir. Any resemblance between me and the bird is purely coincidental."

SUMMING UP

Each business house, each business man, indeed each person has an image. It is an image he creates. He can maintain and improve it, or he can let it deteriorate.

A good image is created by qualities like trustworthiness, honesty and dedication. Negative qualities create a negative image.

A brand is the impact on society that a man's or an organization's image makes.

Air-India had positive qualities to begin with, so it had a good image. In time it became a brand favoured by many travellers. When the image got tarnished, the brand started being disfavoured.

JRD Tata is an example of a man who created a good image of himself and of the Tata House, which became a brand.

Self-Check Exercises

1. Write in three sentences what you understand by an image.

   (Space for answer)

2. State in three sentences how an image can become a brand. Give two examples, from your general knowledge, of famous international brands. For each example you give, write a sentence how and why it became a famous international brand.

   (Space for answer)

7

Brands have Cash Value: Can be Sold and Bought

A brand, though not tangible like a cake of soap or a motor car, has value in money terms. It has an unwritten promise of quality and performance based on empirical data and is, therefore, marketable.

Examples abound of brands being bought and sold without any tangible asset changing hands. One of the latest, announced in late January 2006, is the acquisition of the *Nihar* brand by Marico Ltd. from Hindustan Lever Ltd. (HLL). Marico has a thriving business in coconut oil and perfumed hair oils, whereas HLL had a marginal presence in this segment and, therefore, decided to exit it. It sold the brand for an undisclosed sum.

Another buyout of a brand and trade mark, announced the same month, was by Ranbaxy Laboratories, the Indian pharma company. Its wholly-owned subsidiary in the USA, Ranbaxy Pharmaceuticals Inc., has bought the brand, trade mark and automated manufacturing equipment of Senetak Plc's proprietary disposable injector. The product helps self-administration of parenteral drugs for emergency treatment of shock and other allergies.

The price paid is not disclosed, but the bulk of it must be for the brand and trade mark. The equipment could have been bought in the market and it was second hand.

Posco's Invitation

Posco, the Korean major setting up a Rs. 52,000-crore plant in Orissa to produce 12 million tonnes of steel per annum, has devised an ingenious way to make its brand name popular. Its officials surprised everyone by welcoming guests at a formal ceremony with its sari-clad Korean employees greeting everyone with *swagatam* and *namaskar*.

Not to be outdone, the male Korean ushers received everyone in Indian dress – *pyjamas* and *sherwani* - requesting everyone in Oriya *aasantu* (please come), *basantu* (please be seated) and *khaantu* (please eat). An innovative way to promote a brand, specially in the context of an agitation and police firing in the process of land acquisition for another steel plant leading to several casualties.

The Ambani Split

One of the more interesting issues in the split between Mukesh and Anil Ambani was the use of the Reliance brand name. A Memorandum of Information worked out by lawyers of the two groups and deposited with the stock exchange says that both groups will be allowed to use the Reliance brand name free of any fee or royalty for their existing businesses.

For Mukesh's group, the rights will vest with Reliance Industries Ltd. regardless of which company of the group is involved. For Anil's group, the rights will vest with Anil Dhirubhai Ambani Enterprises and all companies of the group will be entitled to use it.

Both groups are allowed to use the legend *A Dhirubhai Ambani Enterprise*, but none of the two can use photographs of Dhirubhai or Kokilaben for promotional or commercial purposes. For religious or charitable purposes, however, this is allowed.

There is nothing to stop Anil from using the legend *An Anil Dhirubhai Ambani Enterprise*. Similarly, Mukesh will be free to use a similar legend using his name if he so wishes.

Before the split, Mukesh as Chairman had used the services of the global design firm *Minale* to draw up a global identity for Reliance since it was entering the fields of petroleum products retailing, infocom and life sciences. The idea was to project that Reliance was moving on from an industrial brand to become a customer-oriented brand.

After the split, Anil used another global design firm, *David A. Aaker*, to design a brand identity covering his group's businesses of entertainment, information, communication, financial services and infrastructure.

Non-Competition Accord

As part of the split, the two also entered a limited non-competition agreement. This covers the existing fields of business, which were clearly partitioned between the two. This means that none of the two would enter a business in which the other exists.

But businesses grow, and both the groups have growth plans. Anil's group has already entered the business of entertainment by acquiring Adlabs and plans the production of films. He is also entering infrastructure and his group was one of the bidders for the Delhi and Mumbai airports' modernization.

Mukesh has started work on a Special Economic Zone (SEZ) in Maharashtra and plans another one in Haryana. There are reports that the SEZ will have an airport, which seems very plausible. Is there a conflict of interest with Anil who had already entered this field by bidding for Delhi and Mumbai airports' modernization?

For such conflicts, there is a provision for arbitration. In case of a conflict, there will be a mutually agreed panel of arbitrators who will select an expert in the area of conflict. The expert will report whether the brand rights of one group or the other have been breached. The idea is to ensure that there are no two airports or two film production companies flaunting the brand name Reliance.

Further, to avoid such conflicts arising, the two sides have agreed to engage a reputed legal firm to work out a model brand manual.

Two Reasons

Such exhaustive, expensive and time-consuming exercises are necessary for two major reasons. *First*, the people who are the consumers should have no confusion about who the producer of the goods and services offered to them is. In time, the comparative reliability and quality of the goods/services offered by the two groups will be established in the minds of the consumers, and they will make the choice according to the image created by the performance of the two groups.

The second reason is that the image created over time by the producer of goods/services has financial value. We have noted earlier that Marico Ltd. has acquired the *Nihar* brand from HLL. The financial value of a brand name can be very substantial in case of reputed products.

Let us realize that Reliance is a company whose market capitalization – that is the market price of its shares held by its 50 lakh shareholders – is among the highest in India. The value of its Reliance brand must be thousands of crores.

Let us take the example of a company that is perhaps equally valuable. A recent study has shown that Tata has a brand value of $ 5.37 billions, or Rs. 24,396 crores!

The Tata brand is owned by Tata Sons Ltd., which charges brand equity and promotion fees from the 33 listed companies of the Tata group. The fees are used to build up Brand Tata.

Tata Brand and Sub-Brands

Of the Rs. 24,396-crore brand valuation, Rs. 11,629 crores is accounted for by Brand Tata alone where the companies and products carry the Tata name – like Tata Steel, Tata Motors, etc. The rest of the brand valuation relates to "Tata with sub-brands." There are, in addition, four Tata companies which do not carry the Tata name. They are Titan, Voltas, Tetly and Trent. Their brand value has been put at Rs. 1,500 crores.

The Tata brand is probably the largest in India (the brand valuation of most companies has not been made and/ or their data are not available). Counting the world's leading brands, Tata ranks 57th which is very high considering that Tata is a recent entrant in the international arena. Indeed, until a few years ago, India was a closed economy whereas American and European companies - Shell, IBM, BAT, etc. — have been operating across the world for decades.

We have in an earlier chapter noted how JRD Tata devoted a lifetime building up the Tata brand. The effort is bearing fruit faster now with a spate of acquisitions, mostly abroad, since 2002. It is slated to become faster now as Mr. R Gopalakrishnan, Executive Director of Tata Sons, has announced that as much as Rs. 1,80,000 crores is lined up for investment over the next 8 to 10 years. The brand value will progressively go up as the investment starts yielding results. The effort will be, Mr. Gopalakrishnan said, to build up not only *Brand Tata* but *Brand India*.

How Brand was Built

Brand building is not merely quality production. Ratan Tata, the present Chairman of Tata Sons, has disclosed in an interview to Vir Sanghvi of *HT Brunch* what pains JRD Tata took to ensure that the Tata brand continued in hands which could ensure its growth.

Ratan discloses that despite carrying the Tata surname (he is the son of Naval Tata), he was not an automatic choice to inherit the empire that the Tatas had built. For a decade from 1961, then 25, he had to work his way through various

Ratan Tata steps into the oversize shoes of the legendary JRD Tata. A caricature by Dhir.
Courtesy: The Hit Parade

Tata companies, including Tata Steel in Jamshedpur where Rusi Mody was the Managing Director. In 1971 he got his first independent charge of a Tata company, NELCO (National Radio & Electronic Company) when it had lost Rs. 600 crores!

In 1981 Ratan was given Tata Industries to run. Still, it was not certain that he would become the next Chairman of

Tata Sons. The frontrunner, Ratan told *HT Brunch*, was Nani Palkhivala. "It was only because he (Palkhivala) became a vocal critic of the Government that Jeh (JRD Tata) thought his political views might become a liability to the Tatas".

Palkhivala & Mody

Next to Palkhivala in contention was Rusi Mody, who as Managing Director had run Tata Steel so ably and under whom Ratan had worked. So well had Mody run Tata Steel and so strong a contender for the top job was he that in the late 1980s JRD Tata decided to give him the top job of TELCO (now Tata Motors) also. But Mody, for some reason that nobody could fathom, started to make disparaging remarks about Sumant Mulgaokar who had run TELCO so far. Mulgoakar was so cheesed off that he refused to hand over charge to Mody.

"Mody was Jeh's favourite," Ratan Tata recalls. But something more happened. Mody was pushed up to become Chairman of Tata Steel and JJ Irani was made Managing Director. Mody started criticizing Irani's handling of the company. Once he walked out of Tata Steel's Board meeting over which he himself was presiding.

JRD Tata, ever vigilant to guard the pristine purity of the Tata brand, took note of all these personal shenanigans. One by one his favourites had made themselves unworthy of the *Tata Brand*. It was the level headedness and quiet persistence of Ratan Tata that won him the day.

This persistence sustained Ratan Tata even after he succeeded JRD Tata as Tata Sons Chairman. He plumped for a small car with a difference and put men on the job to design it. "Foreign small or medium-sized cars are meant to be self-driven," he told Vir Sanghvi in the interview. He wanted a reasonably small car that could be driven by a chauffeur.

The cost went on rising but Ratan won't give up. After hundreds of crores had been spent on the design alone, many started calling it "Ratan's folly". He continued to persist and sank hundreds of crores more. Ultimately after Rs. 1700 crore had been sunk into the venture, the *Indica* emerged.

TELCO, which had been started to manufacture locomotives for the Railways, became Tata Motors. A bigger car, the *Indigo*, was launched, both cars feeding both domestic and foreign markets. It is one of the major contributions to brand building.

How Brands Yield Crores in Tax

Brands are valuable not merely to their owners, they yield substantial revenue to the exchequer.

Finance Minister Chidambaram's 2005-06 budget brings transactions in intellectual property into the service tax net. If a company buys the use of a brand from another company, it is buying intellectual property, for which it has to pay service tax.

On this principle, Skoda Auto India, which assembles Octavio Multi Utility vehicles near Aurangabad in Maharashtra, is liable to pay service tax since it uses the brand of Skoda Auto of the Czeck Republic and pays royalty for it. Already, Skoda Auto India has paid Rs. 9.1 crores, according to a report on February 9, 2006.

On the same principle, Hyundai Motors India, a subsidiary of Hyundai of Korea, has already paid Rs. 8.5 crores and will have to go on paying on future production.

Eicher Motors of India pays royalty to its technical collaborator, Gaer Eicher of Germany, for using its patented technology. It has already paid Rs. 4 crores and will have to go on paying on future production.

VAT Demand

There is more. Delhi's Value Added Tax (VAT) department is targeting several businesses similarly placed. Under the VAT Act, specific goods and services meant for sale and having a selling price are treated as commodities and are subject to VAT. According to the VAT Commissioner, using a brand for sale is subject to tax. So, businesses like Domino's Pizza outlets, McDonald's and Nirula's which are franchises and pay for using the brand name must pay VAT.

Also liable to pay tax, according to the VAT department, are brands like Delhi Public School (DPS). How? It is explained that DPS has over 50 schools affiliated to it, so it too should pay tax.

Even cricketer Virendra Sehwag, who is paid lakhs to sponsor various commodities, is a brand, so he must pay VAT on those earnings.

SUMMING UP

A brand is an unwritten promise of a specific level of quality and performance. As such, it has value in money terms and can be sold and bought. One of the biggest issues in the split between Mukesh and Anil Ambani was which of the two owns the Reliance brand. It was decided that both can use the Reliance brand name for the existing businesses they had inherited without payment of fee or royalty. For a new line of business, whichever of the two groups enters it first can use the Reliance brand name.

The Tata brand's value has been computed at $ 5.37 billion, or Rs. 24,396 crores. One of the key issues in the succession to JRD Tata as chairman of Tata Sons Ltd. was who could preserve, protect and enhance the brand's value. On this consideration, Nani Palkhivala (his political views) and Rusi Mody (his tendency to be hypercritical of colleagues) fell by the wayside and Ratan Tata became the successor.

Brands mean value in money terms not merely for their owners, the exchequer earns crores by way of service tax (where a brand is used by a franchisee by paying royalty) and VAT (where a brand name is used to enhance the value of a service or commodity).

Self-Check Exercises

1. Write why brands have value in money terms.

   (Space for answer)

2. How can the state tax transactions in the use of brands?

   (Space for answer)

8

Crucial Role of Vision in Management

Management is the art of making things happen. Unless you know what you want to happen, you cannot make it happen.

Knowing what you want to happen is vision. It can be as small a thing as switching on the electric lamp. It can also be the creation of a plant to provide light and power to a whole city.

You know that you want the electric lamp to emit light, so you press the switch button and there is light. Yet, until a century and a half ago, man did not know that pressing a switch botton could make a lamp emit light.

Physicists had by then shown that passing an electric current through metal could make the electrical energy get converted into heat and light energy. The greater the resistance to the passage of the electric current, the greater the heat and light. Acting on this knowledge one man made the electric current pass through a very thin metal wire. There was light. The electric filament lamp was born.

That man's name was Thomas Alva Edison. He had the vision that other scientists possessing the same knowledge did not have. Like all pioneers over the ages, he believed that if something was logically possible, one could always devise a way to make it happen. He had only to persist. Here is a famous saying of Edison which every man who makes a thing happen implicitly believes in.

> *Many of life's failures are people who did not realize how close they were to success when they gave up.*

Edison did not give up, therefore he became the Father of the Electric Filament Lamp.

Every country and every era produces individuals with vision. Had it not been so we would still be living in the Stone Age.

Indian Visionary

In our own country and in our own time, there was a man named Dhirubhai Ambani. The elderly among us were his contemporaries. He was born in 1932, only two years before millions like me were born. He was also, like me, the son of a schoolteacher. His first job, like the first job of many a son of a schoolteacher, was that of a petrol pump attendant, the attendant whom we take for granted when we go to the pump for fuel for a vehicle.

But this petrol pump attendant had a vision. He would create petrol pumps instead of being only an attendant. How to do it?

Venugopal Dhoot, Chairman of Videocon, and himself a visionary, tells us how Dhirubhai did it. He pioneered the equity cult in India, developing the Indian capital market.

Before this, the capital market had been the rich man's playground. Dhirubhai made the small man with small savings invest small sums in it. The money thus collected was put to use to create wealth, then the wealth was distributed among the small investors by way of dividends and bonus shares. The poor man who had only 100 shares in the company found one fine morning that he had suddenly 200 shares thanks to a bonus issue.

The first bonus issue and the first big dividend that Dhirubhai-Ambani made his company declare was an unmistakable communication to the small investor that he could become big, the poor could become rich. On Dhirubhai's death, his company Reliance issued a full page advertisement saying.

> *" For many Indians who said 'I want...', there was one man who dreamt, 'of course, why not?' "*

By the time he died, there were 50 lakh ordinary men and women constituting the huge family of Reliance investors. By this action, he rejected the belief, long held in Indian society, that ordinary men and women were destined to remain helpless. Instead, he communicated the message that the ordinary man need not remain helpless. There was a way to get out of this helplessness.

Dreamers and Day Dreamers

Many, indeed most, people have dreams. When the dreams are out of proportion to the possibilities as seen by ordinary men, it is called building castles in the air. Dhirubhai showed that there is nothing wrong with building castles in the air, only you should have the capability and persistence to lay the foundations – the persistence that Edison had and others had not. The man who has the capability and the persistence is called a visionary. Those who do not have these qualities are day dreamers.

Dhirubhai was a visionary. When a man says "I want..." many call him a man with demands on society. Dhirubhai's response would be "Why not? Let's do it." That's the difference between a dreamer and a visionary.

Another major difference between the mere dreamer and the visionary is this. When there is a low ebb in our affairs, the mere dreamer's dream is shattered. Kamlesh T. Mody of K.Thakorlal and Company, who was an associate of

Dhirubhai for three decades, says when there was a low ebb in his affairs and a crisis loomed, Dhirubhai would invariably look for ways to convert it into an opportunity. This is called mental virility.

There are always several facets of a situation. The visionary takes note of the unfavourable facet and tries to counter it. Simultaneously, he looks at the other facets to see which has scope for an opportunity. In fact, using this opportunity itself frequently helps one get over a crisis.

Business Volumes

Mody tells of another *mantra* of the visionary's success formula. "He encouraged me to increase business volumes," Mody says. A profit of one rupee per transaction over a lakh of transactions means a gross profit of Rs. 1 lakh. A profit of Rs. 10 per transaction over 1,000 transactions would mean a gross profit of only Rs. 10,000. Which would you prefer?

When the West Asian oil producing countries formed the cartel O.P.E.C. and made the price of oil spurt by restricting production, there was consternation among entrepreneurs around the world, for all industrial production is dependent on oil. It was then that Dhirubhai entered the field of oil refining, building the world's largest refinery in Jamnagar. Later, when exploration for oil and gas was opened to the private sector, Dhirubhai entered this too. Many called it building castles in the air. But Reliance has struck India's largest gas field off the Andhra coast. By 2010 or so it will have laid the foundations to that castle and promises to flood south-eastern India with gas to fuel industry and run power stations.

Amitabh Bachchan, another dreamer who built castles in the air and went on to lay the foundations, had this tell-tale comment to make when Dhirubhai died.

I first met Dhirubhai when I had a problem. In fact,

Our dreams have to be bigger.

Our ambitions higher.

Our commitment deeper.

And our efforts greater.

This is my dream for

Reliance and for India.

now that I reflect, barring the odd & social meeting, I have met him only when there has been a problem."

When the problem was explained to him, says Bachchan, Dhirubhai would "analyse, dissect and give a solution in such a simple down-to-earth manner that I felt foolish not having looked or thought of it that way myself."

The visionary does not get bogged down by a crisis. He does his best to meet it, and this doing his best invariably includes looking at other facets of the situation that might yield an advantage.

Silver Spoon

There is no law that visionaries should be born with a silver spoon in the mouth. In fact, as a rule they don't have a silver spoon in the mouth at birth. Instead, they create silver spoons.

The petrol pump attendant of the 1940s died in 2002. but he had laid the foundations for his Reliance Industries to create thousands of petrol pumps all over India. It is the vision of the petrol pump attendant coming true.

Dhirubhai was only a matriculate. After school in Chorwad, a village in Saurashtra (Gujarat) where his father was a teacher, he left aged 17 for Aden where elder brother Ramniklal was employed. He got a job as an attendant at a Burmah-Shall petrol pump.

From what we know of Dhirubhai, he made up for his lack of formal education by dreaming. As one wag wryly commented, he spent three quarters of the time dreaming but made sure to spend the remaining quarter translating his dreams into reality. The result is India's largest business conglomerate built up from scratch within his lifetime.

When the Lifetime Achievement Award was conferred on him in 2001 by the *Economic Times*, the theme of his thanksgiving response was : *Dream and Dare.*

Four-Point Formula

"I dream of an India becoming a great Economic Superpower," he said. For this he prescribed a four-point formula:

"*First*, we must know the problems, " he said. But "it is even more important to know the solutions." For this, "let us acquire knowledge and apply it."

His *second* point was: "We must respect creators of wealth." No social scientist has articulated this in such plainspeak. He described the existing social situation as–

The farmer is dismissed as illiterate.

The worker is condemned as a troublemaker.

Business men are labeled as crooks.

Those who do not produce wealth discredit those who create wealth.

This attitude kills the productive spirit. A society which condemns creators of wealth will always remain poor and miserable.

Trust Creates Initiative

The *third* point he made was: For centuries Indians have been brainwashed to distrust other Indians. The solution : We must learn to trust. Distrust kills initiative. Trust and transparency stimulate entrepreneurship.

We must learn the difference between a mistake and a crime.

Fourth, we must always go for the best. Do not compromise on quality. Reject if it is not the best – the best not only in India but globally.

"Reliance is built on these principles. These are the principles that can help us build a Greater India."

This was on August 10, 2001. Less than a year later, on July 6, 2002. Dhirubhai was no more. These four points were, thus, a virtual Dying Declaration.

First Memorial Lecture

A year later, the First Dhurubhai Ambani Memorial Lecture was delivered by Dr. APJ Abdul Kalam, President of India.

Dr. Abdul Kalam reiterated Dhirubhai's principle "to think big, think fast and think ahead." In Dr. Abdul Kalam's words—

"Dhirubhai Ambani represented a strong mind which propagated that having small aims is a crime."

His actions, Dr. Abdul Kalam said, "gave courage to the small entrepreneur to think big and work towards it." He quoted Dhirubhai's wife Kokilaben as telling her son, "Your father has gone to Heaven. That is his permanent home. God sent him to earth on a mission.....Now there are others to carry on the mission here, so God needs him back in Heaven to carry out His work."

Dr. Abdul Kalam's comment : *Mission makes the man.*

He quoted Tamil saint-poet Thiruvallur who wrote 1330 Kurals (couplets) 2,000 years ago on how to live a good life. "Wherever there is an indomitable spirit of man," he quoted the saint-point as saying, "the man succeeds, the woman succeeds, the village succeeds, the country succeeds, the world succeeds."

"Dhirubhai had a mission, and for success in any mission what we need is an indomitable spirit."

The indomitable spirit has two components. The first component is that there should be a vision leading to higher goals of achievement. Dr. Abdul Kalam quoted another Thiruvallur couplet as saying "whatever may be the depth of a river or lake or pond, whatever may be the condition of the water, the lily flower always comes out and blooms."

Similarly, if there is a definite determination to achieve a goal even if it is impossible to achieve, the man succeeds "This is one of the components of the indomitable spirit and it applies to Dhirubhai Ambani."

Second Component

The second component of the indomitable spirit is referred to in yet another Thiruvallur couplet quoted by Dr. Abdul Kalam. Those who have gone through large programmes and projects must have experienced that oftentimes success is not in sight and there are many hurdles–hurdles created by man, hurdles created by the nature of the programme, hurdles created by technology.

All this is possible in a major programme like wealth generation. But the poet reminds us in another couplet that successful leaders can never be defeated by problems. They become the master of the situation and defeat the problems.

President APJ Abdul Kalam delivering the first Dhirubhai Ambani Memorial Lecture.

"I consider these two Thirukurral characteristics the indomitable spirit of Dhirubhai Ambani," the President remarked. "Whenever he encountered problems, he gave a problem to the problems. He exhibited the indomitable spirit by successfully implementing complex missions."

Satellite Launch

From his own experience, Dr. Abdul Kalam cited an example of the leadership quality. In 1973, Prof. Satish Dhawan, heading the Space Commission, gave him the task to build a launch vehicle to put a satellite into orbit.

The launch vehicle had 44 sub-systems and thousands of components. Thousands of engineers and 19,000 others had worked on it. In 1979 the vehicle was ready and was taken from the Vikram Sarabhai Space Centre to the Sriharikota launch site.

On August 17, he as Mission Director with other scientists was ready to launch it. At T minus 8, that is 8 minutes before launch time, he entrusted the task of checking to the computer since it is impossible for a human Mission Director to check all the hundreds of parameters.

At T minus 4, that is within the next four minutes, the computer said "don't launch", even though the rocket system, the explosive system, the propellant system and the electronic system were "live".

What had happened was that the computer had detected a problem in the second stage control system of the four-stage rocket.

Dr. Kalam consulted his experts, experts with 10 to 20 years' experience in their fields. They advised against obeying the computer. After agonized consultations, Dr. Kalam decided on going ahead as he put the rocket in the manual mode.

It began as a "beautiful launch", Dr. Kalam remarked. The first stage had done its job. The second stage took over, and within a second the rocket went into a spin. Another few seconds, and instead of going into orbit the whole system plunged into the Bay of Bengal !!

At the scheduled press conference soon after, Prof. Satish Dhawan took Dr. Abdul Kalam along. One of the hundreds of national and international media men asked, "How can you put Rs. 20 crores into the Bay of Bengal?"

Dr. Dhawan Response

Dr. Dhawan replied, "Yes, we had a failure". As head of the space programme, he owned responsibility for the failure and added, simply and with conviction. "But we will succeed."

The fault was rectified and, one year later, on July 18, 1980, the launch was organized. Dr. Abdul Kalam was again Mission Director.

It was a perfect launch. The first, second and third stages worked as planned, the fourth gave the escape velocity to put the satellite into orbit.

Thirty minutes later Prof. Dhawan took Dr. Abdul Kalam to the usual press conference. He publicly took responsibility for the first launch's failure but gave the credit for the second's success to Dr. Kalam and his team.

Leadership Quality

"This is leadership quality," Dr. Abdul Kalam remarked in his Dhirubhai Ambani Memorial Lecture. "He switched my failure to his failure" but gave credit for the success to the Mission Director.

"One of the very important ingredients for the success of the vision of transforming India into a developed country by 2020," Dr. Kalam said referring to the long-held time frame he has set for the project, "is the evolution of creative leaders."

What are the qualities of the creative leader? "The creative leadership exercises the task to change the traditional role from commander to coach, from manager to mentor, from director to delegater."

The creative leader is one who changes oneself "from one who demands respect to one who facilitates self-respect. The higher the proportion of creative leaders in a nation the higher the potential of success of a vision like that of a developed India."

SUMMING UP

Management is the art of making things happen. For this, one must know what he wants to happen. Such knowledge is called vision.

To translate vision into reality, one needs persistence. One also needs mental virility, which means the capacity to convert a setback into an opportunity.

(See also Guest Chapter 1 : **A Karma Yogi who lived the Gita** by Anil Ambani.)

Self-Check Exercises

1. Write two sentences about the role vision plays in management.

   (Space for answer)

2. List two contributions made by Dhirubhai Ambani to the development of entrepreneurial culture in India.

   (Space for answer)

9

Different Patterns of Communication

Despite the shining examples of JRD Tata and Dhirubhai Ambani, and of Dr. APJ Abdul Kalam and his illustrious predecessors and Gurus, Dr. Vikram Sarabhai and Prof. Satish Dhawan, there is no single formula for the use of communication as a tool of management. Even within this group of eminently successful practitioners of management, there is wide disparity.

Likewise, there have been other successful managers who have got things done using different models and modes of communication. Hence, there is no "right" or "wrong" pattern of communication .The acid test is what works.

The variations are because human beings are different, situations are different, and the market situation and external environment are almost always different. In the context of India's variable political climate, public policies of the day swing sometimes appreciably, making it necessary for the communication pattern to vary from time to time.

Relaxed Environment

JRD Tata is credited widely with having reinforced the Tata brand and got it entrenched after Sir Jamsetji had taken the initial steps to establish it. He and his contemporaries were working in probably a more relaxed environment than is to be found today.

Tata Steel was the first heavy industry to be established in India in modern times. There were other industries, mainly British-owned, but they were lightweights. The Indian companies were mainly trading houses.

It was mainly at or about partition in 1947 that a large number of British-owned industries came to Indians. The Tatas had, therefore, little or no competition in the areas they operated in.

Tata Steel was the lone major steel maker until the public sector plants came up at Bhilai, Rourkela and Durgapur in the late 1950s and early 1960s. Tata Consultancy Services was for many years the only major Indian IT software company. It is still the biggest. Infosys, Wipro and the others are a comparatively recent phenomenon despite the hoopla.

Air-India, though publicly owned but run by JRD Tata, was a monoply.

Ingenious System

The Tata House devised an ingenious system of management to be effective. The top boss for each company of the group was chosen fastidiously, briefed carefully how he had to be the most efficient and comparable to world standards, and then left to manage things. Communication from and to Tata Sons Ltd was, therefore, minimal and mostly directed at the top boss in each segment.

The Tata Empire, therefore, became a string of satrapies, Rusi Mody produced the world's lowest cost steel at Jamshedpur. Ajit Kerkar ran Bombay's showpiece Taj Mahal Hotel, which in time became a chain spread over India and abroad. Darbari Seth ran Tata Chemicals most effectively. Sumant Mulgaokar's Telco was the monopoly manufacturer of metre gauge steam locomotives for the Indian Railways.

At Air-India, with which JRD Tata probably interacted the most since he was a frequent flier and a flying enthusiast, the Operations Director was the boss. Once in a while JRD Tata would point it out if something was causing inconvenience or discomfort to passengers, and it was promptly set right.

Adi Godrej, Chairman of the Godrej Group, recalls a significant incident of long, long ago, showing how involved JRD Tata was with Air-India. "Jeh had been invited," Godrej recalls, to dinner one day at the Godrej family home. Also invited was Adi Godrej's fiancee whom he was to marry later.

"As soon as Jeh was introduced to her," Godrej recalls, and learnt that she was an air-hostess, he was curious to know what air-hostesses and other airline employees thoughts of the national carrier. "He spent the rest of the evening with my fiancee", remarks Godrej.

Maharaja's Pranks

SK Kooka, as the airline's Commercial Director, had a free hand to invent the Maharaja and make him do exciting things to amuse the passengers. There were occasions when strait-laced members of Parliament protested at the Maharaja's mischievous pranks, but Nehru stood by him. It was a matter of commercial viability and prudery will not do, so Kooka must have the necessary elbow-room.

The system of satraps worked in JRD Tata's time. It was only when Ratan Tata became Tata Sons boss that dissent developed. For one thing, most of the satraps were senior to Ratan. Rusi Mody had been the top boss at Tata Steel when Ratan had been put there to go through the mill.

He ran Tata Steel admirably without so much as a distracting sound from the staff or anyone. Even the Steel Town functioned as a model of contented camaraderie.

Mody was not only the top boss, he was considered a beloved senior fellow worker at Tata Steel. He could go into a throng of workmen and charm them into warmly welcoming him.

All this changed when Mody was pushed up by JRD Tata as Chairman of Tata Steel and JJ Irani became Managing Director. Modi was critical of Irani's handling of the Tata flagship.

But the fact was that JRD Tata had higher responsibilities in mind for Mody. He nominated Mody to take

Russi Mody who produced the finest steel at the lowest cost for Tata steel. A caricature by Dhir.
Courtesy: The Hit Parade

over Telco also. Here again Mody made a hash of it. He started criticizing Sumant Mulgaokar's handling of Telco!

Had the Peter Principle taken over? The Principle, propounded by Prof. Peter, says that every worker reaches the Level of his Incompetence. It is cited in the same breath as Parkinson's Law - that work expands to occupy the time at the worker's disposal. A third celebrated sociological law of management is that if anything can go wrong, it will. It is called Murphy's Law.

Peter Principle?

Did the Peter Principle become operational? Mody had been the model of competence as Managing Director of Tata Steel. When pushed up to be Chairman of Tata Steel and simultaneously the top boss of Telco, had he reached the Level of his Incompetence?

One would never know. For, many things intervened. The JRD Tata era ended. Ratan succeeded him as Chairman of Tata Sons Ltd.

Inevitably, Ratan took time feeling his way. He thought restructuring was due. He entrusted the job to the in-house Tata Strategic Management Group. One area identified was soap and detergents which TOMCO (Tata Oil Mills Company) was producing. It was only an also-ran to Hindustan Lever Ltd (HLL), the market leader in this segment. Even the American giant Proctor & Gamble was eyeing a prominent role.

It was decided to sell TOMCO to HLL. Even as TOMCO was going to HLL, Darbari Seth at Tata Chemicals was planning a foray into detergents and soaps. Seth, along with Mody, was senior to Ratan, perhaps too senior to heed that the Tatas were exiting soaps and detergents!

Another senior was Ajit Kerkar, the hospitality czar presiding over the Indian Hotels (Taj Mahal, etc) empire.

Telco had switched from metre gauge steam engines since the Indian Railways were phasing out metre gauge. It was now big time into manufacturing trucks and buses, first in collaboration with Mercedes-Benz and then on its own.

Tata Cars

The exciting new segment was automobiles, which seemed a natural twin to Tata trucks and buses. Ratan plumped for developing a car indigenously instead of going in for collaboration with an established foreign car-maker. He set the ball rolling. Crores, then hundreds of crores, were sunk into the project. In time the wizened veterans started calling it "Ratan's folly".

Ratan now took another momentous step. The Tatas had no policy on retirement for the top bosses. He got Tata Sons to prescribe a retirement age.

All the seniors were past or approaching this age. Rusi Mody went kicking and screaming. He had spent 54 years at Tata Steel, made it produce the finest steel at the lowest cost and was 75. He set up a trading company of his own.

Centaur Episode

Kerkar was next. His Taj Mahal Hotel and its chain were the glamorous face of the Tatas. He thought of it as his own baby. He too retired.

Perhaps giving the message, like Mody, that it was the Tatas' loss to release him, he went into the hospitality business again. Floating a new company, he bought the Bombay Centaur Hotel, which was owned by Air-India and was now being privatized. Some time later, his newly floated company sold the acquired Centaur property at a huge profit.

So far we have been talking of how communication can be, and has been, used as a tool of business management. Politics also uses communication as a management tool. It is assumed that politics as a rule uses communication to ask business "what is there in it for us?" Buddhadeb Bhattacharya has turned this assumption on its head by telling business, "look, here is something for you"- and that something has turned out to be what business wants.

Welcome by Gherao State

For three decades West Bengal was the gherao state. It became common for industrial workers to start demanding a cut of the fruits of production long before the fruits came, and sometimes regardless of whether or not there were any fruits. As a result, existing factories stopped production and new investment stopped coming.

Bhattacharya reversed this trend. Investment was welcomed with open arms, with the promise that tools like gherao will not be employed.

The response was hesitant to begin with. Closed factories started getting reopened. Then a number of IT (Information Technology) companies ventured in. The Salim group of Indonesia was allowed to set up industrial and residential townships.

Enter Tatas

The latest big catch is Ratan Tata's Rs. 1-lakh car project for which a large tract of the land is being acquired. Following the Tatas, Videocon with its consumer durables and the Jindals are trooping in. Now Mukesh Ambani's Reliance has come up with its Rs. 3000-crore project to set up a retail agro-products chain with facilities in every district.

The trigger was Buddhadeb Bhattacharya's unconditional communication welcoming industries and promising a congenial atmosphere for production and growth. If there is a medal for using political communication for good economic management, it must go to the far-seeing Chief Minister of West Bengal.

Jyoti Basu's Stand

And why only Buddhadeb Babu? Even Jyoti Basu, who as Chief Minister fathered the gherao culture, has changed his stand. Asked by a reporter why the Left's strike call for June 13,2006, in protest against the fuel price rise had paralayzed Left-ruled Kerala but didn't affect West Bengal, he said: "They (Kerala) saw an advantage out of the total strike so they went for the strike. Here, we thought a five-minute *chakka jam* and street-corner meetings would register our protest."

In fact, a few days after the call was given for the strike, the state CPM had announced it would restrict it to token protests. "I don't want to send wrong signals to investors," Buddhadeb Babu had said.

Full Attendance

So strong is the state party's support to Buddhedeb Babu's stand that the state Assembly, whose session began on the strike day, adjourned after the obituary references as is customary, but reassembled soon after to continue its business. The state secretariat, which is completely unionized, recorded full attendance of ministers and staff.

Smooth Transport

Even the transport sector, including state-owned buses, functioned normally in Kolkata and other parts of the state. No road or rail services were stalled anywhere.

Further, Buddhadeb Babu's Cabinet colleagues and senior bureaucrats worked out details of the land acquisition plan for the state's FDI projects of Indonesia's Salim group, since representatives of the group were to arrive in Kolkata next day.

Such is the communication that Buddhadeb Babu and his Government have given to investors.

SUMMING UP

Although there can be no management without communication, there is no fixed formula to be applied. There is no right or wrong pattern of communication. The acid test is: if it works, it is the right pattern.

For a long time, the Tata companies were run by a string of highly motivated and competent satraps. Each was autonomous, with Tata Sons Ltd, the parent company, exercising loose control. Communication was between the satraps and the Tata Sons Chairman, who was JRD Tata. The arrangement worked.

When Ratan Tata became Tata Sons Chairman, the benevolent presence of JRD Tata was missed. There was inevitable unrest. Many of the satraps were senior to Ratan and there was resentment at the erosion of autonomy.

Retirement Policy

Ratan made Tata Sons formulate a retirement policy for the top management. The seniors had to go. This, together with the success of the indigenously designed and developed automobiles, led to closer integration and more meaningful communication between Tata Sons and the units.

Even as these changes were taking place, Bengal Chief Minister Buddhadeb Bhattacharya set a new benchmark in political communication leading to good economic management of his state by inviting investment. Investors, including the Tatas, who had given up on West Bengal, came flocking in, showing that even political communication can be used as a good management tool.

Self-Check Exercises

1. Describe the system of satraps that prevailed in the Tata group in JRD Tata's time.

   (Space for answer)

2. What was the political communication sent by Buddhadeb Bhattacharya that managed to reverse the business trend in West Bengal?

   (Space for answer)

10

Dhirubhai Ambani Pattern of Communication

Dhirubhai Ambani's rags-to-riches story is by now part of the folklore of Indian business. But how this was achieved is a vague blur on the popular radar. This is how it happened.

He had arrived in Aden aged 17 and taken up the job of a Burmah-Shell petrol pump attendant at Rs. 300 per month. He rose fast and became sales manager. The next move up was to be a merchandising clerk at a Burmah-Shell associate firm named A. Beese and Co. Salary: Rs. 1,100 per month.

Many in 2006, when the lowliest peon earns Rs. 5,000 in India, would think Dhirubhai was a poor man with a low salary. But costs were much lower in the 1950s. I remember to have bought a kilogram of ghee for Rs. 6 in 1961. Today it costs Rs. 150 or more.

Comfortable Lifestyle

Dhirubhai had a car and a flat and all that goes with these things. Magistrates in India those days had the same salary and maintained a car and a comfortable lifestyle.

But Dhirubhai threw it all up and returned to India after eight years on December 31, 1958. He had with him his toddler elder son Mukesh and his wife Kokila pregnant with their second son Anil. Not for him a laid back lifetime in an alien land to return home 30 years later as a prodigal son who had made good abroad. It was too unexciting.

Usme Nasha Hai

Years later, at a lunch with K K Malhotra, head of Reliance's manufacturing operations at Patalganga, he bared his heart's yearning. He ordered soup and a *papad.* Malhotra had a one-egg omelet. As they nibbled at the food, Dhirubhai remarked: "This is all we need, right? But the excitement is to build.. ..*Usme nasha hai.*"

It was the quest for this *nasha* that had brought him back to India in Bombay. He had a few thousand rupees in savings. With this money he bought yarn from mills and sold it to powerlooms to weave. He made a profit and lived from day to day.

Was this a downmarket existence? Years earlier in village Chorvad, recalls elder brother Ramniklal, Dhirubhai when only 13 or 14 would get together with some friends and sell *ganthia*, a Gujarati delicacy, during the *Mahashivratri* fair.

Adds a Chorwad contemporary, "Dhirubhai was a familiar sight, cycling from village to village. All he needed was a business opportunity and he was off to book orders."

Kabutarkhana

As a yarn trader now in Bombay, Dhirubhai rented a flat in a chawl in Kabutarkhana in downmarket Bhuleshwar. The building was named Jai Hind Estate. There, on the fifth floor of the chawl, was located his one-bedroom flat. In that flat lived the whole Ambani family having migrated from Chorwad – Dhirubhai, his wife and two small sons, his mother Jamna and a younger brother. His father Hirachand had died when he was 19 and in Aden, not yet married.

It was a "pigeonhole type" flat - 20 such flats on one floor. There was a long corridor running along the flats. Nearby was a temple. Residents of the flats would go to the temple to pray. On coming out, they would throw part of the *prasad*, which was *chana* or gram, for pigeons to eat (feeding birds is considered an act of piety among Hindus). So, at temple time, hundreds of pigeons would converge on the locality, hence Kabutarkhana!

Dhirubhai earned what anyone less ambitious would consider a comfortable living. Was he to end up as a trader buying and selling yarn? Never, he vowed. "I wanted to start a company like Burmah-Shell," he admitted many years later.

Trading Firm

He rented a small office in Bhaat Bazar and started a trading firm named Reliance Commercial Corporation. He had nursed his connections in Aden, which was a free port under British rule. Since the hinterland was all desert, Aden imported all kinds of commodities for consumption free of customs duty. This brought good money to those who supplied these goods.

The manufactured goods mainly came from Britain, so Dhirubhai concentrated on exporting agricultural goods growing plentifully in India - ginger, cardamom, pepper, turmeric, cashewnuts, sugar, ghee, etc.

Roses in the Desert

Once a Sheikh expressed a desire to grow roses in his desert fiefdom. Why not, said Dhirubhai. He scooped up a shipload of fertile Indian soil and exported it to the Sheikh!

With his export business doing well, Dhirubhai broadened its scope. Under a new Export Promotion Scheme, one could export rayon fabrics and import from the proceeds nylon yarn which sold in the Indian market at a premium of 15% to 30%, frequently more. Dhirubhai entered the trade. "You do not require an invitation to make profits," he was to remark later.

With new horizons visible, Dhirubhai floated Reliance Textile Corporation. He would manufacture textiles.

The norm those days was, however, that you could not manufacture 100% filament synthetics except on powerlooms. Dhirubhai applied for and obtained a licence.

The drill was to buy yarn from outside and weave "greys" or unfinished fabrics. The "greys" were sold to processing houses, which processed and printed the cloth and sold the unbranded fabrics to wholesale traders. These traders would brand it and sell it in the market at a substantial premium.

Backward Integration

Dhirubhai's business brain started ticking. Why manufacture "greys" and sell them at low prices for processing and printing to others who made a fat profit from them?

This was the start of his backward integration *mantra*. He would process and print his own "greys" and reap the profits. Backward integration has since then become the trade mark of Reliance. The slogan "Only Vimal" was about to be born.

To set up his textile manufacturing unit, Dhirubhai needed capital. He approached various friends and associates. Among them was Viren J. Shah, Chairman of Mukand Iron and Steel.

Shah belonged to a family which was the biggest landowner in Chorwad village. Dhirubhai had asked for only Rs. 400,000. But Shah turned down the request. "The project will not work," he is reported to have remarked.

Instant Hit

Dhirubhai was not one to be deterred. He arranged the money anyhow and set up his textile mill at Naroda near Ahmedabad.

The project was an instant hit. In the very first year, 70 workers manning four wrap-knitting machines and a small dyeing section notched up sales of Rs. 90 lakhs and a profit of Rs. Rs 13 lakhs. By 1977, the year Dhirubhai went public by making his Initial Public Offering (IPO), the mill had revenues of Rs. 70 crores and a profit of Rs. 4.33 crores.

Until this time his main sales were in exports. Mills were allowed to import polyester filament yarn against the export of nylon fabrics. But the scheme under which this was permitted ended in 1978.

Dhirubhai promptly turned to the domestic market with an advertisement blitz on billboards, radio and print. The campaign for "Only Vimal" was so big that it startled everyone. It compared with the biggest launched by FMCG (Fast Moving Consumer Goods) majors like Hindustan Lever.

Message to Consumers

This mighty advertisement blitz was meant to communicate a powerful message to consumers, a message that they could not forget. "Only Vimal" became a household term.

The prospective customers had been alerted. The next step was to reach the product to them. Typical of him, Dhirubhai's attack on this problem took the form of another blitz. The traditional distribution channel preferred the products of old, established mills. There was a reluctance to take the produce of a new, untried mill.

Two Prongs

Dhirubhai proceeded to establish a new channel of distribution. There were two prongs of it. The first prong was to open "Only Vimal" showrooms. This was not something new. Others had tried it before. Nusli Wadia of Bombay Dyeing had opened exclusive showrooms for his products with considerable success. Delhi's DCM also had a chain of exclusive showrooms doing well.

Dhirubhai, even while opening "Only Vimal" showrooms, buttressed the campaign with a very innovative effort. He toured the length and breadth of the country, offering franchises to Reliance's newly recruited army of shareholders. To those who agreed and had the shop space, Reliance promised financial and advertising support.

Crucial Three Years

For three years between 1977 and 1980, one Reliance outlet would be opened almost everyday. One particular day in 1980 saw almost 100 outlets being opened in various parts of the country. By 1980 Reliance fabrics were available all over India through 20 company-owned showrooms, over 1,000 franchisee outlets and 20,000 regular retail stores.

One of the oldest Reliance marketing managers who took part in this campaign says the *mantra* was to tell the franchisees and retail outlets that "doing business with us is risk-free. If you lose, come back to us. If you make profits, they are yours."

The big, established mills concentrated on the metros and the big cities. Some went to big towns also. Reliance fabrics, through the distribution blitz, reached deep into the non-metro urban areas also.

Ingenious Solution

Very soon, as a direct result of this distribution blitz, Reliance's entire production capacity could not meet the burgeoning market demand. Dhirubhai set about devising ways to solve this problem.

The Government policy was not to allow more looms in the big mills. Licences for additional looms would be granted only to powerlooms. Somebody in the Government apparently thought this would create more jobs. Dhirubhai devised a solution to this problem. Reliance went on replacing the older and slower looms with the faster looms that advance in technology had enabled industry to produce. So, with the same number of looms Reliance produced more fabrics.

Simultaneously, Dhirubhai remembered what small powerlooms used to do in the early days. They would manufacture "greys" and sell them to processing units for finishing and printing, and the finished product would fetch fat prices in the market.

So Reliance started buying "greys" from the small powerlooms in Bhiwandi, Satara and other places, finishing and printing them, and feeding the finished product to the ever hungry market. Reliance's production, availability in the market and sales zoomed.

Links with Shareholders

Establishing a rapport with customers through a widespread customer network deep into big and small towns was one part of Dhirubhai's communication pattern. The other part, which was equally crucial and fruitful, was to establish strong links with shareholders.

So long as Dhirubhai's company was a private one, he hardy ever treated himself to a dividend. All the profit was ploughed back into the business. With the 1977 IPO, Reliance became a public limited company. In the first year itself, Dhirubhai declared a dividend of 15 per cent.

Next year. 1978, there was a slight dip in profit, but the dividend was scaled up to 27 per cent. Had Reliance gone off its head? Not at all. The sharp increase in dividend was a pointed message to shareholders: When you invest in Reliance, your money earns rich returns.

Dividend plus Bonus

The message was doubly reinforced one year later. In 1979, the dividend was 25 per cent. In addition bonus shares were issued in the ratio of three shares for every five held.

There was sensation in the market. Word spread among shareholders that Reliance was a gold mine. Everyone in the market made a beeline for Reliance shares. As a result, the price of the share appreciated by 450 per cent.

Promptly Reliance announced an issue of partly convertibe debentures to finance a worsted spinning mill. It meant a guaranteed return on one part of the investment and Reliance shares in lieu of the other part. The issue was oversubscribed by six times. Every year for the next three years Reliance issued debentures - in 1980 for modernizing the textile mill, in 1981 to finance PFY manufacture, a record Rs. 500 crore in 1982.

This reinforced the message sent out from 1979 onwards (when there was a 25 per cent dividend plus a 3:5 bonus issue) that when Reliance invites investment it uses the money wisely and promptly and rewards shareholders handsomely.

'Reliance Family'

Dhirubhai spoke of the Reliance Family every time he received a national or international award during the next two decades - and there were more than a score of such occasions. Accepting the Indian Businessman of the Century Award conferred after a worldwide multimedia poll conducted between August and October 1999 by *Business Barons* magazine, he said: "My fulfilment lies in the satisfaction of every member of the Reliance Family, comprising thousands of workers, managers, business associates and over five million shareholders. Being instrumental in creating wealth for over five million Indian families, and bringing prosperity and well-being to their life is the deepest source of satisfaction and joy for me."

The poll, which received over 41,000 valid votes from as far away as North America and Australia, selected him as the leader from a list of 10 nominations. He received the

Indian Businessman of the Century

The Ten Giants

Sr. No.	Businessman	No. of votes
1	Dhirubhai Ambani	10,142
2	J.R.D. Tata	9,126
3	G.D. Birla	4,940
4	Aditya Birla	3,855
5	Jamnalal Bajaj	3,717
6	Ratan Tata	3,450
7	N.R. Narayana Murthy	1,812
8	Azim Premji	1,710
9	Walchand Hirachand	1,501
10	Kasturbhai Lalbhai	1,304

Source: Results of global multimedia poll between August and October 1999 to identify the ***Indian Businessman of the Century – the industrialist who had the greatest influence on Indian business in the last 100 years*** *– Business Barons.*

maximum number of votes, 10,142, which is about 25 per cent of the total valid votes polled. Only JRD Tata with 9,126 votes came anywhere near him. Each of the rest polled less than 5,000 (see chart).

Ford and Gates

The magazine, reporting the results of the poll, compared Dhirubhai's achievements to some of the greatest business initiatives in the industrial history of the world. "It is an achievement that ranks alongside - indeed perhaps outranks – Henry Ford's founding of the Ford Motor Company and Bill Gates's founding in the 1970s of Microsoft," it said. The reason it gave was that "both Ford and Gates had inherent advantages: greater resources when they began their careers, no red tape and a developed industrial infrastructure and markets. Dhirajlal Ambani had nothing - except that extraordinary fire which lit his every move and eventually led him to build a formidable, globally competitive industrial machine.

Shareholding Habit

Appropriately, Reliance is credited with spreading the shareholding habit in India. Before Reliance's mega issues, the Bombay Stock Exchange raised about Rs. 1.7 billion in the year 1980. By 1990 it was raising the same amount in a week.

Before Dhirubhai spread the equity habit, it was customary for businessmen to raise loans from banks started by the Government of India and dedicated to finance big business activities, like the Industrial Development Bank of India (IDBI), to set up or expand businesses. It was unimaginable that retail investors with small amounts of a few thousand rupees of their hard-earned money would entrust it to a businessman starting out to establish or expand a business.

Funds Denied

Since Dhirubhai had risen within a few years from being a small-time yarn trader, such loans were routinely denied to him by the financial institutions. It was this that made him turn to the small investor. Today it is calculated that out of every four retail investors in the share market, one holds Reliance shares.

Having opened this new channel of getting funds for investment, Reliance has borrowed heavily not only in India but abroad to finance its phenomenal diversification and expansion into petrochemicals, telecom, infrastructure, etc. In 1992 it became the first Indian company to issue Euro Global Depository Receipts, followed in 1994 by a second Euro issue. This is apart from repeated public issues for shares and debentures in India. The biggest public issue in India is that of Reliance Petroleum made in April 2006.

In January 2000, Dhirubhai was voted the topmost Creator of Wealth of the Century in the Indians of the Century online poll conducted by the *Times of India*. The Reliance group had created wealth of Rs. 73,000 crores and had emerged as the largest wealth creator among Indian business houses. Of this, Rs. 49,000 crores was shared widely by 50 lakh retail investors.

Father of Stock Market

The report of the poll described Dhirubhai as the Father of the Indian Stock Market who had imparted respectability to wealth creation. His belief in enhancing shareholder value goes back to a time when the term was unfamiliar to the Indian public, it added. His *mantra* was *Think Indian, Act Global.*

Reacting to this report, Dhirubhai reiterated his familiar assertion that "the honour should go to the members of the Reliance Family - the five million investors who reposed their trust in me to build Reliance, the 20,000 employees who devoted themselves to make Reliance happen and the thousands of consumers who made Reliance grow."

Indians of the Century

The result emerged from the online *Indians of the Century* poll conducted under four categories: 1. Leaders and Politicians. 2. Great Minds and Spiritual Lights. 3. Artists and Entertainers. 4. Creators of Wealth. A total of 8,81,772 voted in the poll.

While Dhirubhai emerged as the Creator of Wealth of the Century, Mahatma Gandhi – who "remains a forceful icon among Indians" – led in the Leaders and Politicians category, Swami Vivekananda – the first of the modern Indian gurus – was selected in the Great Minds and Spiritual Lights category, and Lata Mangeshkar – a cultural phenomenon of our times – was selected in the Artists and Entertainers category.

"A close look at the top four names suggests several shared characteristics", the report said. "All of them are self-made individuals, they did not have the advantage of wealth, aristocracy or caste; they fought adversity and believed in action – *karma yogis* in the true sense. They made India proud and gave the world new ideas, dreams and hopes."

Family of Shareholders

Ten months after this, in November 2000, the Chemtech Foundation and Chemical Engineering World called Dhirubhai the creator of the Largest Family of Shareholders in the World. This was in recognition of his pioneering effort in the petrochemicals industry, which was virtually non-existent in India before this.

Dhirubhai's Response

Responding, Dhirubhai said: "I am proud to be part of the chemicals industry. It has made a great contribution to economic development. It has played a great role in improving the quality of life of the common people It has a great past and, I believe, a greater future."

Dreamer or Doer?

Then he proceeded to disabuse his admirers of a notion that they had expressed. "Friends often praise me for being a doer," he said. "In fact, I take pride in being a dreamer. Big achievements follow if you dream big. Reliance is proof of the power of dreams.. ...Reliance is also the message behind that name. I have always believed if you rely on people, you can do wonders. Trust them. You can achieve miracles. Lakhs of people have joined me in building Reliance. Between us there has always been one common bond: reliance and trust. They placed trust in me. In return I stood by that trust, without wavering. Reliance is a triumph of trust."

There is an interesting sidelight to this. It is customary to hold the Annual General Meeting (AGM) of companies in halls hired from hotels. But the result of Dhirubhai's blitz to add shareholders was that Reliance could no longer hold its AGMs in a hotel hall since there were far too many shareholders attending. So Reliance had to hold its AGMs in huge football stadiums.

A Paradox

Reliance thrived in the pre-1991 controlled economy. It has thrived even more and grown faster in today's liberalized economy. This is a paradox that has foxed many.

One person who has resolved the paradox is Arun Shourie. As Editor of the *Indian Express*, he had in the pre-1991 period published carping criticism of Reliance by S. Gurumurthy and others for routinely producing more than the capacity for which its plant was sanctioned. Such critics thought it was a breach of regulations.

After Dhirubhai's death in 2002 Shourie, who had become Minister of Disinvestment in the NDA Government, acknowledged the mistake. He realized that producing more than the capacity for which a plant was installed was not a crime. It was a feat to be admired and emulated.

Ingenious Ways

In the above account, we repeatedly see instances where Dhirubhai devised ingenious ways to make his plants produce more than the capacity they were installed for.

Weaving plants, including powerlooms, have a sanctioned number of looms. Dhirubhai bought and installed faster looms as they became available with improvement in technology and replaced the old, slower looms with them. The number of looms remained the same but production increased. The catch is to mistake the number of looms allowed for production capacity. The size of a mill may be prescribed in the licence. But this does not and cannot prevent it from producing more through hard work, more intensive use of plant, using improved technology or through other ingenious devices.

Here is another instance. When market demand for Reliance textiles outstripped supply, Dhirubhai bought "greys" from the smaller powerlooms, processed, printed and branded them and fed the market. This is not illegal and lots of mills were doing it. In fact it was the norm for the smaller powerlooms installed in garages to sell their "greys" for others to process, print, brand and sell. Yet, when Reliance did it, there was an outcry that it was producing more than the sanctioned capacity.

Another Secret

Another secret of Reliance's success Dhirubhai once revealed. "I wasn't the only one to get licences. But just because the Government gives you a piece of paper it doesn't automatically mean you can mint money from the market, put up a plant in record time, and give sensible returns to shareholders. That's 98 per cent of the work. The paper work is only 2 per cent."

One more secret of his phenomenal success was revealed by Dhirubhai when he admitted that "I do not give attention to anything except Reliance. I am not a director in any other company. I am not actively participating in any association or anything else."

Like "Only Vimal" for Reliance customers for textiles, it was "Only Reliance" for Dhirubhai Ambani.

SUMMING UP

Dhirubhai started life as a 17-year-old petrol pump attendant in the then British-controlled free port of Aden. Rising rapidly, he became Manager of the petrol pump. He had a car and a flat but returned to India on December 31, 1958.

Starting as a yarn trader in Bombay, he kept his communication links with Aden open. He exported ghee, cardamom, cashewnuts, etc., to associates in Aden, making good money. Once he even exported a shipload of fertile Indian soil to a Sheikh who wanted to grow roses in the desert!

Setting out to manufacture cloth, he got a licence for a powerloom unit. He was clear in his mind that he had to communicate intensively and extensively with retailers and franchisees. He toured the country and built up a chain of some 20,000 outlets – "Only Vimal" showrooms, franchisees and retailers.

With Shareholders

His next aim was to communicate with prospective shareholders. He made an Initial Public Offering (IPO) in 1977 and promptly declared a dividend of 15 per cent. Next year's dividend was 27 per cent. In 1979 he declared a dividend of 25 per cent plus a 3:5 bonus.

Word spread in the share market that Reliance was a gold mine. The share price appreciated by 450 per cent. This was followed by repeated issues of debentures, etc.

This is how he built up the world's "largest family of shareholders", as a Chemtech Foundation award was to say. There were many more awards – the Indian Businessman of the Century, the Largest Creator of Wealth in India, etc.

But Dhirubhai remained modest. His mantra was *Think Indian, Act Global.*

Self-Check Exercises

1. Why did Dhirubhai Ambani return to India despite leading a comfortable life in Aden? What reason did he give for doing so?

   (Space for answer)

2. Describe how Dhirubhai created "the world's largest family of shareholders".

   (Space for answer)

Reliance - Major Milestones – I

1977
First IPO to the Indian Public

1982
Launched Phase 1 of the Polyester Filament Yarn (PFY) Plant

1985
Entered Phase 2 of the Polyester Filament Yarn (PFY) Plant

1986
Started the Polyester Staple Fibre (PSF) Plant

1986
Started PTA Plant

1987
Started the Linear Alkyl Benzene (LAB) Plant

1988
Started the PX Plant

1991
Launched Phase 1 of MEG Plant

1991
Set up the Vinyl Chloride Monomer (VCM) and PVC plants

1992
Commenced the production of High Density Polyethylene (HDPE)

1992
Offered the first ever Euro Issue of Global Depository Receipts by an Indian company

1992
Set a record with Reliance Twin issues that received over 1 million investor applications

1993
Sales crossed Rs. 4,000 crores making Reliance India's largest private sector company

1993
Offered the first Euro Convertible bond issue

1993
India's largest public offering – Reliance Petroleum Issue

1994
Offered the second Euro issue of GDR

1995
Net profit crossed the Rs. 1,000 crore mark (Rs. 1,065 crores or US$ 338 million), unparalleled in the Indian Private sector

1995-96
Reliance became the first private sector company to be rated by international credit rating agencies. S&P rated BB+, stable outlook, constrained by the Sovereign Ceiling. Moody's rated Baa3, Investment grade, constrained by the Sovereign Ceilings

Reliance - Major Milestones – II

1996-97

Completion of Rs. 9,000 crore (US $ 2.5 billion) Hazira complex increasing production capacity from 1.5 million tonnes to more than 6 million tonnes

1997

First corporate in Asia to issue 50 and 100 years bond in US debt market

1998

Following plants commissioned
80,000 tpa bottle-grade PET plant
120,000 tpa MEG plant
350,000 tpa PTA plant
200,000 tpa PE plant

1999-2000

Jamnagar Petrochemicals complex and bulk of integrated refinery complex commissioned comprising:
World's largest grassroots refinery
Indis's largest port with capacity of 50 million tpa
World's largest PX Plant of 1.4 million tpa
World's largest PP plant of 0.6 million tpa
Captive power plant of over 300 MW
World class product handling, storage, and despatch facilities

2000

Started commercial production of 27 million tpa refinery, the 5th largest in the world

2000

Increased stake in BSES by an open offer

2000

Launched share buyback program

2000

Reliance infocom plans annonced

2001

RIL and RPL become India's two largest companies in terms of all major financial parameters

2002

RPL's merger with RIL to create India's first and only private sector Fortune Global 500 company

2002

Reliance acquires government's 26% stake in IPCL, Indis's 2nd largest petrochemicals company

11

Hero Group's Multi-tier Communication Model

Unlike JRD Tata, who had inherited a six decades old giant steel business and expanded and diversified it, the Hero Group started from a bicycle retail shop in Ludhiana. The cycles were made by other companies, mainly British. The shop only sold them.

Brij Mohan Lal Munjal reasoned that no bicycle could remain in good health for ever. Each unit would need to replace worn out parts from time to time. The big problem was of quality. As everyone who owns any kind of machine knows, a large proportion of the spare parts available in the market are either spurious or substandard. Original parts made to strict quality specifications are not easily available, or are available at far off places.

Troublesome Problem

For bicycles this is a particularly troublesome problem, since hardly anyone checks his vehicle for functionality while at home except for punctures. Most malfunctioning is detected during journeys away from home.

In India of those times, the bicycle was the preferred vehicle for personal journeys with small loads. For big loads, it was the bullock cart. Motorized commercial or personal vehicles were rare.

In cities and towns one could find cycle repair shops. In rural areas no repair shop would be available for miles. Even if one could find a shop, one could not be sure of the quality or durability of spares. So the Munjals took steps to manufacture quality parts which could be relied upon.

The venture was successful. So, when the Punjab Government decided in 1956 to issue licenses to manufacture whole bicycles, the Munjals applied. They got one out of a dozen licenses issued. Hero Cycles was born.

10 Crore Bicycles

Fifty years later, on June 2, 2006, the company held its Regional Dealer Conference for the Northern Zone and Chief Minister Amarinder Singh was invited to the ceremony to roll out its 10 croreth (100 millionth) bicycle made in the five decades of its operation.

The Munjals' was, let us remember, one of a dozen licenses issued 50 years ago to manufacture bicycles. One reason for Hero's success was, of course, the quality and sturdiness of its machines, though it is certain that none of the dozen licensees could have made fragile bicycles by choice.

The key reason why the Munjals succeeded whereas the others did not must have been the quality of the communication to its customers, dealers, workers and other business associates.

Guiding Principles

Like Reliance's three-tier communication model, Hero's has more than one tier. First, Hero's product must be sturdy. The bicycles must be rugged, giving confidence in their strength, particularly in rural areas. Secondly, they must be widely available, even in small towns. Thirdly, and this is vital in any trade, their parts, genuine and custom made, should be always and easily available in the farthest comer of the country where customers operate the company's machines.

How did the Munjals manage it? First of all, there was – and always has been – a rare unity of direction in the group. Whether it was the late Dayanand, the founder, or Brij Mohan Lal, the Chairman, and the two Co-Chairmen, elder brother Satyanand and Om Prakash, who is the youngest of the brothers and also Managing Director, there has always been unity of vision and direction.

Zero Defect

The guiding principles have been "just in time" and "zero defect." The first refers to all operations being so coordinated that no subsequent operation has to wait. The second means identifying problems before they reach the customer. So, if there is any defect in the procedure of production, or in the product itself, it is always the company that identifies (and therefore rectifies) it, never the customer.

This may sound too theoretical but has had a remarkable effect. Starting with 25 bicycles a day, the company today manufactures 16,500 a day. It is the largest cycle manufacturer in the world and is in the Guiness Hall of Fame. It is also the largest exporter of bicycles. Its products are to be found in the markets of 82 countries across the world, including such advanced manufacturing nations as the USA and Britain and, in fact, in all of Europe.

Remarkably, Hero has always thought ahead of its time. This generation, and even the one that preceded it, will not realise it, but there was a time five decades ago when all bicycles were black – just as all negroes are born black or all South Asians grey (often called brown).

Many Innovations

What's wrong with the colours, asked Hero. Finding no reason to stick blindly to black, the company produced cycles in other colours - and they sold. Likewise, it produced cycles custom-made for ladies and children, and they were also immensely popular.

Today Hero has 100 models of cycles in various categories. In the Roadster category it has 20 models including Hero Jet and Royal. The kids segment has about two dozen models.

Hero is all set to launch bikes of the future. The eco-friendly Hero Power runs on batteries and is poised to take cycling beyond transport, sport and recreation. Besides, as part of its anniversary, Hero proposes to bring two unique products - Hero Octane, a globally competitive aluminum alloy bicycle, and Hero Cyclomoto, an engine-driven bicycle.

As O P Munjal says, "the future belongs to those who see reality and convert it into opportunities."

Scooter Revolution

While the Munjals were conquering the bicycle market came the motor scooter revolution. Bajaj made Vespa scooters with Italian collaboration and API made Lambretta with another Italian collaborator. Bajaj won with Vespa's superior technology, graduated to Chetak, a machine more powerful than Vespa.

India seemed to have been conquered for ever by Vespa, and later the same company's Chetak and Bajaj models. The waiting list to take delivery of a scooter rose to tens of thousands, with a waiting time of years.

But the Munjals had other ideas. They entered into technical collaboration with Honda, the world leader in motor-cycle technology. The idea caught on, for Honda brought vastly better fuel-efficient and super-silent technology. More significantly, the communication line for consumers was that motor-cycles were macho. The youth fell over each other to grab a Hero Honda motor-cycle.

Ancillary Units

Not only this, the Hero Honda company opted for the practice of encouraging the creation of ancillary units with strict adherence to technical specifications. Another forward step was vendor development - a key step not given great importance in India until then. The *mantra* until then had been an integrated plant which carried out all the production functions. Those who wanted the product had to find out who and where the seller was.

Pioneer

Vendor development has been employed with a revolutionary impact by Dhirubhai Ambani (20,000 retail outlets for "Only Vimal"). Maruti, in collaboration with Suzuki, has also employed the strategy of vendor development and creation of a large number ancillary units for its cars. But both these came later. The Munjals were the pioneers in the field.

The impact of these two strategies was dramatic. First, motor-cycles became the heart-throb of India's youth, replacing scooters. As a result Bajaj, the scooter king of the country, had to enter into collaboration with another Japanese company to produce its own motor-cycles.

Hero Honda became the motor-cycle king of India. Runaway sales led to runaway profits. For the third year running, it announced a dividend of 1000 per cent for the year 2005-06 – Rs. 20 dividend on each share of the face value of Rs. 2.

Two More Plants

There are two plants running, one in Dharuhera and the other in Gurgaon. A third plant is already coming up in Jaipur to become operational soon. Next year, yet another plant will come up, so insatiable is the hunger for Hero Honda motor-cycles.

At Hero Honda, communication is two way. Even as the company announces growth plans, it has its ears cocked to listen to consumers' suggestions and demands. As a result, eight new models, each incorporating one or more of customers' suggestions, are planned in the next two years.

SUMMING UP

The Hero group started its journey from a shop selling bicycles in Ludhiana. Bicycles need spares like all machines when their original parts wear out. As everyone knows, many spare parts in the market are substandard or spurious. Brij Mohan Lal Munjal thought up a solution to the problem. He would manufacture spare parts with strict quality control so that bicycle-owners do not get cheated.

This was the start of the group's journey. During this journey it has made 100 million (10 crore) Hero cycles in 50 years.

Scooter Companies

Meanwhile, motor scooters had entered India. Two companies from Italy, which was the world leader in scooters, entered into technical collaboration agreements with Indian companies. The products they put in the market were Vespa and Lambretta.

Vespa, made by Bajaj, became more popular because of its technical superiority. The waiting list went into tens of thousands and the waiting time years. India seemed to have been conquered by scooters for good.

The Munjals, with a firm foothold in bicycles, thought up a solution. Scooters in India were using technology imported at the time the technical collaboration had started. Technology had advanced much since then. Fuel efficiency was vastly better now, and the machines had drastically cut down on the noise level. Such technology was already in use in motor-cycles. The Munjals entered into technical collaboration with Honda, the world leader in motor-cycles

Along with technology came modern commercial practices. The Munjals vigorously promoted the development of ancillary industries. A vast and vigorous vendor development programme was taken up.

Hero Honda has kicked up India's motor-cycle revolution. The scooter empire has been vanquished. For the year 2005-06 the company declared a dividend of 1000 per cent for the third year running.

New Models

The revolution has not yet reached its zenith. The company has two plants running but they are not able to feed the burgeoning demand. A third plant at Jaipur (the earlier two are at Dharuhera and Gurgaon, both in Haryana) is being built and will be commissioned very soon. The fourth plant is being planned. As part of its communication with consumers, the company will incorporate customers' suggestions and requirements in eight new models it plans to launch in 2006-08.

Self-Check Exercises

1. The Hero Group's rise from the grassroots to the present pre-eminence in the two-wheeler sector is characterized by a continuous two-way communication with consumers. Describe how.

   (Space for answer)

2. Give reasons why motor-cycles were able to vanquish the scooter empire in India.

   (Space for answer)

12

Positioning and Other Subtle Management Tools

The layman's idea of management is barking orders to be obeyed. In the chapters so far, we have seen that management is much more than that. JRD Tata created a string of satraps, leading to the creation of India's biggest industrial empire of its time, by communicating largely with the satraps only. He is not mentioned in the voluminous literature on his life and times as having ever barked orders. In fact, there is no record of his having lost his temper.

Dhirubhai Ambani pioneered a three-tier communication strategy to build up an industrial empire within three decades – the "Only Vimal" advertisement blitz aimed at consumers, the massive 20,000-outlet nationwide network for his fabrics, and the "reward shareholders" campaign to build up the world's "largest family of shareholders", as the Chemteck Foundation calls it.

Communication Process

Communication, in fact, is the process of passing on a message which is so coded as to be understandable to the receiver so that he can respond. If he responds favourably, the message has acted as a tool of management. If he has not, it is the job of the communicator to so code his message, or send such a message, that the response is favorable and the communication acts as a management tool.

There are subtler methods than orders, methods that are equally effective as a management tool. Prof. Subroto Sengupta, Visiting Faculty at IIM Kolkata, identifies positioning as a management tool. According to him,

"...... *positioning is the strategy of occupying a place in the consumer's mind which sets your brand apart from others despite its functional similarity. It imbues the brand with a distinctness that attracts a given customer segment.*"

Lest anyone dismiss this as semantics, there is the example of cars. All cars are a means of transportation. Yet some are positioned as entry level vehicles (e.g. Maruti-800), others as limousines, still others as SUVs.

Many Segments

There are seven or eight segments in which motor vehicles are positioned, and each segment is almost wholly exclusive. Or else, why would Governments or other organizations opt for wholesale replacement of, say, Ambassador cars by better positioned vehicles like Innovas or Land Cruisers?

New Cars

The latest example is the campaign of the impoverished Nikhil Kumar Government in Bihar to replace all Ambassador cars used by the Chief Minister and other Government VIPs.

For Nikhil Kumar, the government is buying five bullet-proof Scorpios. At present he makes do with two bullet-proof Ambys. For the ministers 26 Scorpios and 26 Indigos have been approved. One minister says many of the present 300 Ambys are "useless".

Nation-wide Phenomenon

An interesting study of this nation-wide phenomenon made by Shobha John for the *Times of India* was published in the issue dated July 2, 2006. Here is a gist of her findings.

In terrorist-prone Jammu and Kashmir, Chief Minister Ghulam Nabi Azad has three Safaris plus a jammer-fitted Amby costing Rs. 1 crore. The Chief Minister is escorted by a dozen cars. The cost to the exchequer is about Rs. 4 lakhs a month.

Punjab's Capt. Amarinder Singh, though belonging to the ex-royal family of Patiala, is not ostentatious. He uses four bullet-proof Ambassadors alternatively for security reasons. His ministers are more stylish and use Camrys costing Rs. 35 lakhs each. MLAs use Qualises costing about Rs. 7 lakhs each.

A Mercedes

The style-*bhai* among CMs, Haryana's Bhupinder Singh Hooda, has a Mercedes-E. The ministers have been given Innovas and the M.L.A.'s Balenos. Both Amarinder Singh and Hooda have cavalcades of six to seven cars.

Delhi's Sheila Dikshit, rough and tough, has a white AC Amby. There was a proposal to give her a more high-profile vehicle but she is comfortable with her Amby. Education Minister Arvinder Singh Lovely says: "As we are on the road 100 to 150 km everyday, this sturdy car is fine." But Finance Minister A K Walia says this car breaks down frequently. Maintenance per car costs Rs. 60,000 a year.

Uttar Pradesh CM Mulayam Singh Yadav travels in style, both in his state and in Delhi. There are eight Prados, three of them bullet-proof - five in U.P. and three in Delhi. Ministers are provided Ambassadors but 150 new cars are to be bought.

Ghosts of Godhra

The ghosts of Godhra seem to drive Gujarat CM Narendra Modi. While cabinet colleagues drive around in Chevrolet Optras, Modi has three Safaris, all bullet-proof.

They were bought for Rs. 18 lakhs each after the riots. He suddenly chooses any one of them while commandos travel in the other two.

In Financial Capital

You might think the CM of the financial capital of India would be ostentatious. But Vilasrao Deshmukh uses only a bullet-proof Amby. The convoy has a Maruti Esteem kept by the police. Ministers now use Ambassadors or Esteems after the earlier Contessas. Some are loaned by corporations and bodies reporting to their departments.

Simplicity Buddha

Simplicity, thy name is Buddhadeb Bhattacharya. The West Bengal CM has an AC Amby. Finance Minister Asim Dasgupta has an ordinary Amby. Other ministers use AC Qualises, AC Esteems and Ambys. In March 2004 the Transport department bought 28 new cars, including 17 LPG-run Ambys, eight Esteems (for guests visiting the state), and three Sumos as some ministers were asking for luxury cars. Frugality is not everyone's cup of tea.

Unlike his father, Naveen Patnaik does not show a passion for hot wheels. His father Biju Patnaik was not just a daredevil pilot but traveled widely in his Kalinga Rath, a custom made Matador. Naveen uses two AC Esteems. Though he owns an Amby, he seldom uses it and prefers to hire a Qualis during elections.

H D Kumaraswamy straddles the old and the new – an Amby with bucket seats costing Rs. 6 lakhs and a Lexus worth over Rs. 25 lakhs. His ministers prefer Mitsubishi Lancers and Skodas. Some have requested for Scorpios and Corollas.

Mercedes Again

The staid Amby is Karunanidhi's official car - he has three of them. His personal liking is more flashy - a Merc and a Scorpio. With Left leanings, he and his ministers are tight with money. During the 1996-2001 tenure, train passengers to Madurai and Trichy often found the CM as a co-passenger. Ministers are given Scorpios while the Chief Secretary has a Honda City.

How will a Leftist CM drive to work? V S Achuthanandan and his ministers make do with 12 new Ambassadors and eight old ones. The only Mercedes is with Governor R L Bhatia.

All Kerala CMs during the past 15 years have used Ambassadors. It is a sign of simplicity, says an official.

Two Brands of Yogurt

Prof. Sengupta, in his contribution to the path-breaking book *Communication-2000* A.D. (published in 1990 and edited by the author of this book) cites the example of two brands of yogurt. Mishti Doi is positioned as a dessert but Milkfood Yogurt's positioning is –

> *Eat it as breakfast... as a mid-morning snack...-with a sandwich for lunch...or even as tea...... it's great as dessert too.*

Management is not merely of the workforce. It is also management of consumers ("Only Vimal"), of distribution (Reliance's 20,000 outlets), of investment, of clients, of public interest campaigns and much else. A very large part of India's population (40 per cent or so who have access to TV) have got hooked to soap operas through a unique campaign to manage the mood of the masses. Yet soap operas are a very recent phenomenon on Indian TV, only 22 years old in 2006 A.D.

Soap Operas

Prof. Arvind Singhal of College of Communication, Ohio University, and Prof. Everett M Rogers of Annenberg School of Communication, University of South Carolina, trace in *Communication-2000 AD* how this mode of management of the mass mood started in 1969 in Peru, spread to Mexico in 1975, and came to India in 1984 with *Hum Log.*

The pioneering soap opera was *Simplemente Maria* in Peru. It spread the use of the sewing machine among the lower middle class through a series of episodes which entertained while they educated. In Mexico, *Ven Conmigo* promoted adult literacy to the extent that enrolment in literacy classes jumped nine times in the one year that the episodes were telecast. Another Mexican soap opera, *Accompaname,* promoted family planning, and within a year contraception jumped 33 per cent.

Indian Debut

The family planning movement in India was flagging, mainly because it was seen as propaganda mounted by drawing room *bhadralok* who had nothing better to keep them busy. Even the idea of marrying it to entertainment did not stir the imagination of many, who thought it would end up as cheap sloganeering for family planning.

But two original thinkers got stuck to the idea -- Dr. Norman Borlaug, Nobel Peace Prize winner for the magic wheat which set off the Green Revolution, and Dr. M S Swaminathan, India's top agriculture scientist. One thing led to another and Doordarshan bosses agreed to air such a serial educating through entertainment. But they had funds and technical capability to produce only one half-hour episode a week.

Following the experience of Peru and Mexico, advertising agencies were consulted, and they agreed that advertising could be marshaled for the programme provided the story line of the episodes was attractive enough.

39 episodes in 40 days

It was then that Manohar Shyam Joshi, a Hindi novelist and editor, who was enthusiastic about the idea, was roped in. He churned out the story line, the character sketches, and the summary of the first 39 episodes in 40 days flat.

Singhal and Rogers record that *Hum Log* commanded audience rating of 65 to 90 per cent in the predominantly Hindi-speaking North and 20 to 45 per cent in the main cities of South India. When the serial ended on December 17, 1985, there were widespread sentimental protests from viewers.

What *Hum Log* had achieved was to manage massive audiences for such public interest issues as family planning, empowerment of women, family harmony and national integration. Today there are dozens of soap operas in India's many languages, focusing on family problems and trying to spread socially wholesome values with varying degrees of success.

Research Report

A similar kind of management of the mass mind is subtly achieved by pure, unvarnished research reports. A lot of protest was recently mounted on research leading to the conclusion that a number of the states of the world are failing in various degrees. The conclusion may be right or wrong, but it does focus attention on the danger.

A UNESCO research report published all over the world more than a decade ago shocked Indian society by asserting that 1.2 crore girl children born each year in the country die by reason of neglect, discrimination or infanticide just because of their sex. The report had been prepared at the request of the Government of India to mark the Asian Year of the Child. Many expressed shock and disbelief at the finding. But it served as a management tool also, for Ela Bhatt, then a member of the Planning Commission, mounted a campaign for better and non-discriminatory public services like health and education.

Sex Ratio

The report proved prophetic too, for it is common knowledge now that the sex ratio even in prosperous states like Punjab and Haryana is skewed against girls and women. Further research has proved the reliability of the original UNESCO report, which was really an alert for better and more equal management of gender issues.

More than research statistics, and probably at par with television soap opera, fiction and films help powerfully to mould and manage public opinion, though their impact is so subtle that most of those swayed by them do not realize it is fiction, not fact. Only this May (2006), a man wearing a string of beads of various sizes robbed a bank of Rs. 40 lakhs in Delhi by telling the manager that the beads were bombs and he was a suicide bomber. When caught a few days later, he confessed he had been influenced by a novel which told the story of a man who had pretended to be a suicide bomber - and succeeded.

Bride-burning

The late Sunil Dutt, who was a much respected film producer-director-actor, and was for many years a Member of Parliament, once produced a film with the title *Yeh aag kab bujhegi.* It was an iconoclastic film talking of bride-burning woven in an entertaining story. But talking to journalists he said bluntly –

> *....the film focuses on the crime of bride-burning.....The problem of women being burnt has been going on in our civilization for thousands of years, only the name of the fire keeps changing from time to time.*

> *In ancient days, Sita had to prove herself in the fire of purity. Then we had the practice of Jauhar, which was followed by Sati. Now we have bride-burning.*

The film, though camouflaged as a story, was an attempt to mobilize and manage public opinion against the evil. Such attempts at swaying public opinion against social evils do have an impact, though this cannot be shown statistically.

Kashmir Sex Scam

There are other such efforts, which have a more visible impact. In April 2006, a reporter of the *Indian Express* in Kashmir unearthed a case of luring minor girls into having sex with influential police, administrative and political persons by dangling before them the bait of well-paying Government jobs. In the beginning it seemed a routine sex racket. But it sparked a massive protest by enraged citizenry, leading to further investigations.

Flesh Trade

It was found that it was the tip of a massive trade in human flesh. The State Government, the CBI and the High Court got involved in digging deeper, and the Prime Minister himself called for a thorough probe sparing no one. A newspaper report of what seemed a routine crime story performed the function of a powerful manager who took on a massive racket in trafficking in human beings and is set to wreck it. There can be no better example of a subtle communication tool triggering a powerful movement against a social evil and worsting it. Any manager would be proud of it.

Family Level

Even at the family level, the awful power of a subtle signal to manage a personal crisis is shown by an episode connected with BJP leader Pramod Mahajan's death. When

Pramod's father Venkatesh had died 35 years ago, his wife was disconsolate and hysterical. Apart from the emotional trauma caused by the personal loss, she felt utterly helpless, left as she was to raise a brood of half a dozen children the eldest of whom was Pramod, barely 21 years old.

Pramod not only managed the upbringing of his minor siblings, he pulled his mother out of her depression. Among the tools he used to manage the feat was singing to his mother the *Mother India* song –

Duniya mein jab aye hain to jina hi padega........
(having been born in this world, we have to live)

When Pramod was shot dead in cold blood in April 2006 by a disgruntled kinsman, the mother broke down crying "Who will sing that song to me now?" Such is the unfailing managing power of subtle communication signals.

SUMMING UP

Contrary to the popular perception that management involves only barking orders to be obeyed, there are also subtler ways of communication which can and are used as a management tool.

One subtle way is positioning a product. Thoughtfully done, it powerfully impacts both production and distribution.

Carefully thought out communication models can be – and are – used as a powerful management tool to mould and direct public opinion against social evils or in favour of wholesome social values. Starting with *Simplemente Maria* (1969) in Peru, spreading to Mexico with *Van Canmigo* (1975) and coming to India with *Hum Log* (1984), the television soap opera has proved to be a powerful medium of communication which has acted to manage the popular mood decisively – and continues to do so. The impact of the tool is subtle but its effectiveness is clear and powerful.

Self-Check Exercises

1. How does positioning act as a management tool?

   (Space for answer)

2. How does the television soap opera act as a tool to manage public opinion?

   (Space for answer)

13

Marcom or Marketing Communication: Final Management Tool

Management, as we have seen, is the art of getting things done. Unless one communicates what he wants done, it cannot and does not get done.

Production is the first and key component of management. Until value is produced, management is stillborn. Immediately after production comes distribution. Unless the value produced is distributed in the market so as to be available to those who want to consume it, production is useless. In other words, the value addition is futile unless and until there is a distribution system to reach it to consumers.

Dhirubhai Ambani, JRD Tata and Brij Mohan Lal Munjal would have been deemed to be failures if they had not created a distribution network for whatever they had produced.

Consumer Awareness

Next to distribution comes consumer awareness about the product. This can amount to image-building or the making of a brand. The Tata brand has been built up to mean excellence in its field. The Hero Honda brand means it is a macho product. The image of the brand must sink in into the consumer's mind.

Consumer awareness is, yet, not the ultimate step in management. The product has rolled out of the factory, it is widely distributed in the market, consumers are aware of its presence, yet there is one more push needed before the consumer opts for it. This step is marketing.

If communication is an essential element of production, distribution and brand-building, in marketing it is the paramount element. It is the final step before the product passes from the producer to the consumer.

Motivating the Consumer

What does marketing consist of? Production, distribution and brand-building have taken place, yet the prospective consumer must feel the need for the product before he goes for it.

Marketing consists of making the consumer realize that he needs it, or that he will be better off acquiring it or worse off by not acquiring it. This requires motivation. If you do not have the motivation, the marketing person can provide it.

The marketing person's job is difficult enough in any situation. The normal assumption is that the consumer knows best what he needs, and it seems logical too. That is why this assumption remained unquestioned in every society for long ever since man became a social being from the freelancer that he must have been at the advent of mankind on earth.

Not Wholly Correct

Empirical data over the years have shown, mainly since World War II, that the "consumer knows best" doctrine is only partially correct – marginally in some cases, more substantially in others, but almost never wholly.

To take a very telling example, insurance companies have two kinds of staff – the account-keepers (clerks in crude language) who keep track of the money, and the field staff who sell insurance. There is no factory, and nothing as tangible as pencils or motor cars is produced.

The cutting edge work force consists of the field staff (insurance agents and their supervisors called development officers). If they were not there, the insurance company would have virtually nothing to do. And what do insurance agents do?

Agent's Role

They convince individuals, groups and companies why and how much they need insurance. If the individual who ultimately gets insured knew he needed insurance and how much of it, there would be no need for insurance agents. Yet, it is the agents who keep the insurance industry going.

This is marketing at its most eloquent. But, less eloquently yet effectively, it works in every sector and every commodity or service consumed. It is the latest addition to the trade of management, and it has yielded rich results.

It is marketing that is leading to globalization. The *mohalla* market is turning into the city market, the city market into the state-wide market, the state-wide market into the national market, and the national market into the global market.

Globalised Ideas

It is not merely physical products that are thus being globalized, it is also ideas. We have seen how the soap opera, purveying education through entertainment, started as a strictly local product in Peru, crossed the national frontier to Mexico, and then migrated thousands of miles to India in the garb of *Hum Log*.

Soft drinks like Coca-Cola and Pepsi, from a product catering to strictly local taste and with avowedly zero nutritional value, have to thank the magic of marketing for becoming a global product. In contrast, freshly extracted sugarcane juice has remained a local product despite its high nutritional value and universal taste. There are a Coca-Cola Corporation and a Pepsi Corporation. Have you heard of a Sugarcane Juice Corporation? The difference is marketing.

Heterogenous Society

Marketing is difficult enough in a homogenous society. It becomes more difficult in a heterogeneous society like India's. There is one national language with an alternative, English, plus a variable mix of the two which is widely used. The bazaar business language is usually a mix of two or more languages - Hindi and English, Hindi-Urdu-Punjabi-English, Tamil-Telugu-English, Bengali-English-Hindi, etc.

The problem is made more complex for the marketing person by the innumerable dialects - 844 at last count. Uttar Pradesh, Uttaranchal and half a dozen other states are characterized as Hindi-speaking. Yet the dialect spoken in Ballia deep in East Uttar Pradesh will be almost unintelligible to the people of Uttaranchal, even though the two states, when they formed a single unit, were ruled for long periods by two Chief Ministers hailing from Uttaranchal. Why, even Uttaranchal has two major dialects, Garhwali and Kumaoni-with several sub-dialects.

The Problem

Internationally, it is not much different. All of China speaks Chinese. Yet the Chinese of Western China is vastly different from Manchurian, which is different from Cantonese, which is Greek in Sinkiang.

The world thought it had solved all the linguistic problems of Central Europe when it carved a tiny state named Czechoslovakia out of the Austro-Hungarian Empire at the end of World War I. Seven decades later, when the iron grip of the Soviet Union loosened, Czechoslovakia agreed to become two separate linguistically homogenous states, the Czech Republic and Slovakia.

The marketer functions in this milieu with communication his only tool. Also, he has no history to borrow ideas from. Until World War II, the norm was for everybody to mind his own business. Anyone trying to tell somebody he needed a particular product was considered an interloper and resented. All that marketing consisted of was for the producer or retailer to try to persuade a prospective customer to buy his product.

Cynical Response

The response often was cynical, for the producer/retailer was seen as trying to earn a profit from a product he had to dispose of anyhow, whatever the quality, or else he would suffer a loss.

Enter the marketer. He has not produced the goods, nor is he the retailer. If he cannot find a customer, he doesn't incur a loss. The job is only to convince a person he will be better off by buying the product or worse off if he doesn't buy.

No wonder marketing is a profession which has been slow to take off. But so was information technology. When Narayan Murthy started Infosys, he could not promise his handful of collaborators a decent livelihood. Or any livelihood at all. He only had an idea.

How Infosys Did It

He set out to sell to big industrial or trading concerns the idea that he could do their problem-solving or backroom work more efficiently and cheaper than they themselves could. The concerns, once convinced, were happy to contract out their work, for the job in which they specialized was very different. Today, tell me who would not like to enter the field of information technology.

Marketing today is at the stage where information technology was a decade ago. Marketers in the whole of India can be counted on the fingertips. Yet the trade is growing, and growing fast.

I know of a person who did an electrician's course, started freelancing, then took up a job as an after-sales man for Aquaguard. Visiting hundreds of homes having Aquaguard water purifiers, and finding that there were a dozen companies making similar gadgets and putting out new models every few months, he started out on a wholetime career marketing these gadgets. He makes demonstrations of new models from house to house and earns a better living than ever before.

Wal-Mart and Others

But why cite individuals alone? What Wal-Mart is doing in America and a dozen other countries is marketing-married-to-retailing. In India, there are Shoppers' Stop and Pantaloon and a dozen smaller marketers with hundreds of outlets. Mukesh Ambani is pitching in with thousands of outlets in Punjab, Haryana and now West Bengal. Sunil Bharati Mittal of *Airtel* fame has set out to procure customized vegetables and fruit produced under contract farming to market in the metros and abroad. The brand is *Farm Fresh*.

Each of these thousands of outlets will need scores of marketing professionals. Each professional will be equipped with nothing more than marcom, or marketing communication expertise.

Differences from Advertising and PR

So far the slot of marketer has been filled up by anyone having an acquaintance with communication of any sort. From salesmen to plain graduates with a glib tongue, anyone is supposed to fill in as a marketer. Many think advertisement executives can be marketers. Others believe public relations

(PR) persons, whose job is image-building for their organizations, qualify as marketers.

However, marketing is different from advertising and public relations. The advertisement person is good at singing praises of his product, regardless of who is (or is not) listening. It is like fishing. You cast the net, and the unwary fish get caught, the clever ones escape.

Public relations persons doing marketing is again a shot in the dark. For, public relations (PR) is aimed at everyone, not at anyone in particular.

Marketing communication means you know enough of both marketing and communication. Inherently, marketing means you concentrate your efforts at a certain audience. It is no use explaining the uniqueness of your brand of car to a crowd of jostling passengers waiting (and cursing) at a bus stop. Along with knowing your audience, you must have the communication skills to convince.

Insurance Company

I am reminded of the Development Officer of an insurance company (inevitably LIC, because insurance had just been nationalized) talking one evening to my father who had just retired as Principal of a college. Since they were friends of some standing, the conversation veered to the concerns of a man retired with four dependent children. At the end of an hour, they had made plans for two insurance policies, one for my younger brother who had just entered college, and the other for my sister who had to get married in a few years.

It is remarkable that the insurance man concentrated on finding a solution for the retired man's concerns, suggesting several alternative solutions. Not once did he commiserate with his friend. In fact, he said that retirement is well-earned rest after a lifetime of labour.

The fact that India with its large number of educated people looking for a job has not many marketers means not that they are not needed but that people who otherwise qualify lack the necessary marketing skills. According to the COO (Chief Operating Officer) of a company specializing in marketing communication, the bottleneck is that many believe a degree is enough for a marketing career and a course in communication is the icing on the cake.

Many Kinds of Communication

The fact is that marketing communication is different. Journalists need one kind of communication skills, actors of another kind (evidence: the National School of Drama and the Film and Television Institute of India or FTII). Publicists for the Government are trained in different kinds of skills to serve a host of organizations like the Field Publicity Division of the I & B Ministry. The communication skills needed for marketing are different.

Every age specializes in and develops different kinds of skills. At one time manufacturing skills accounted for the greatest amount of value addition, sparking the Industrial Revolution. Now these skills are being transferred from Europe to China and India.

The new skills which will lead the world are trade and knowledge creation. It is not accidental that convergent trade issues led to the creation of the European Economic Community, and then the European Union. The process spread to South-East Asia (ASEAN) and North Africa (NAFTA or North America Free Trade Association). South Asia is struggling to evolve a similar institutional mechanism (SAFTA).

Heavily Dependent

Trade is heavily dependent on marketing communication. It is notable that an increasing number of persons who lead national political currents are coming from trade and marketing. French statesman Maurice Schumann was the father of the European Common Market, predecessor of the European Union.

More than reservation crusaders or foreign policy experts, who are proliferating, India today needs marketers. For, after some degree of proficiency in industry, every society needs people who can market what is produced. They have to be imparted special communication skills needed by marketers.

SUMMING UP

Management is the art of getting things done. One has first to manage the production of value, then its distribution in the market, then the spread of consumer awareness of the product or brand-building. The last step in the process is marketing, that is, convincing the consumer that he will be better off if he opts for the product and worse off if he does not. This is done through marketing communication, or marcom.

A shining example of marcom is the insurance agent. He does not produce the object he markets, yet he produces value both for his company and for the object of his attentions.

Marcom is the last step in the management of business. Its importance is that all the earlier steps become stillborn if the product does not reach the consumer.

Marcom promotes both tangible objects and ideas. The Coca-Cola and Pepsi worldwide empires are the product of marcom. So are the education-through-entertainment TV soap operas like *Hum Log*.

In recent times marcom has led to path-breaking political transformations like the European Economic Community followed by the European Union.

India needs hordes of marketers but has still too few of them. This is because awareness is lacking that to become a successful marketer one needs special training in marketing communication. It is like special training in other specialized areas of communication, for instance journalism, acting, public relations and advertising.

Self-Check Exercises

1. Do you agree that marketing communication is necessary to complete the management process of production-distribution-image building and marketing?

   (Space for answer)

2. Advertising, public relations and acting need different kinds of communication skills. How is marcom different from them?

   (Space for answer)

14

Five Mandatory Communication Mantras of Management

Business transactions involve more than one party. One party gives something, the other gives something in return. When any of the two does not fulfil its part of the bargain, no transaction takes place.

The aim of management is to make transactions take place. If this does not happen, there is no business. Management has failed.

In legal terms this is expressed as "there is no contract without a consideration." If a man says "I will give you Rs. 500", it is only an expression of intent. There is no deal. But if the wording is "I will give you Rs. 500 for the new bicycle you have given me" it is a contract enforceable in law.

I.O.U.

Likewise, when one says "I owe you Rs. 500", it is a contract, for implied in this statement is that the other party has already given him value worth Rs. 500, whether in cash or kind. In legalese, this is called I.O.U. (Short for "I owe you)"

There are five norms to be followed if transactions are to take place and business is to prosper. If any or all of them are not followed, business does not take place, or withers and dies. These are called the *Five Mandatory Communication Mantras of Management*. Here is the first one:

Communication *Mantra* 1 of Management

Response : Management must respond to all business communications in good time.

All business communication are sacrosanct if transactions are to take place. This is because there are two parties.

Communication may be oral, in writing, by gestures, or in any other way. It may be direct or indirect, explicit or implied. Written communication everyone understands and need not detain us here. But consider the following:

Company X orders Printing Press Y to print a given text into 1,000 greeting cards to be delivered to its Manager at 10 a.m. on December 1.

On November 30, Y is told that the Manger of Company X has left on a sudden summons from the Managing Director to meet him in Delhi, which is 1,000 miles away.

When and Where

Should Y still deliver the cards at 10 a.m. on December 1? It yes, where to deliver, at the Manager's residence or at this office? It not, then when and where to deliver?

It is not necessary to respond by the mode by which the communication was received, but respond one must.

There are two major reasons why one must respond. First , the party that made the communication needs to be certain that the communication has been received. Letters can be lost in transit or delayed. Even at the communicator's end, the Dispatcher of Company X might have gone home by the time the letter was typed and signed, and so the letter might be sent one day late.

If the communication is oral or by gestures, the communicator needs to be assured that it has been received.

The second reason is that it is necessary, and sometimes vital, for the communicator to know that his communication has been correctly decoded and understood.

This is why it is necessary to give a recognizable response. It is not all right to keep mum when the Manager of Company X says that he is going out to meet the boss in Delhi. Printing Press Y must, in such a case, respond by seeking a clarification whether the cards are still to be delivered on time, and where.

Second Requisite

The second major requisite of this *mantra* is that the response must be given in good time. An author I know once sent the manuscript of his book and did not get an acknowledgement from the publisher even three weeks later. He spent sleepless nights and ultimately made frantic trunk telephone calls, to which the publisher replied, "Your manuscript is under consideration."

Was this a timely or adequate response? In such a weighty matter, a bland acknowledgement, with a note that the manuscript's consideration will take a week (or a fortnight or a month), is necessary. Remember, the transaction is in the interest as much of the publisher as of the author.

Communication *Mantra* 2 of Management

Specificity : All management communication should be as specific as possible.

All of us have noticed that Government communications are frequently vaguely worded. Most official communications, whether public or bilateral, promise action "as soon as possible", or "in due course" or "in the course of time". Such vagueness is the enemy of good management. No wonder our country is mismanaged.

Politicians' Reasons

Politicians and officials avoid being specific because in many cases they are themselves not sure of the time frame, or of the certainty of being able to do the job. In any case they are not personally involved or interested.

Professional managers, on the other hand, have to be interested in the transaction taking place, otherwise no business takes place – and business is their bread and butter.

Printing Press Y, therefore, must couch its response as "the cards will be printed and ready on December 1." Even more desirable is to specify the time "....will be printed and ready at 3 p.m. on December 1."

It is desirable to specify the time and place of delivery even if these details had been settled when the contract was signed. This is desirable so that the other party is reminded to be ready to take delivery at the appointed place and time. It saves on misunderstandings and builds up mutual trust, which is necessary for business to prosper.

Communication *Mantra* 3 of Management

Share Information: Share all the information you have about the progress of the work with the other party.

When a contract is entered into, the party ordering the goods/services and the party that is to deliver them have an equal interest in information about the execution. It is particularly necessary to share information in cases where the execution of the contract is contingent upon the happening of something beyond the control of the parties.

Here is an example. Sometimes the party that is to manufacture the goods does not routinely stock the raw material. He has to obtain it from the wholesaler or the importer on receipt of an order. Even if the raw material is not routinely in short supply, no one can be certain that the wholesaler or importer can provide it at all times.

Uncertainty

The raw material may be on the high seas and may reach the importer after two days. Or the wholesaler is still waiting for the material he ordered from the mill/mine to be delivered.

The manufacturer and the wholesaler/importer will of course keep in touch over this. If the manufacturer is told of any delay, he must intimate it to the party that placed the order with it. If later this delay is made up for, it is the duty of the manufacturer to keep his client informed. Half the disputes between manufacturer and client take place because information is not shared in time.

Communication *Mantra* 4 of Management

Never cut Corners: Once a deal is made, it is in the interest of both parties to honour its terms both in letter and spirit.

Many business deals are made through negotiations. Even where deals are entered into through bids, as happens in most deals entered into by the Government, negotiations are not uncommon. For the Advanced Jet Trainer meant for the Indian Air Force, bids were invited. Those who bid for the contract included a Russian, a British, a French and an Austrian manufacturer.

Even when the British bid, made by British Aerospace for the Hawk trainer plane, was chosen in preference to the others, negotiations went on for a decade on the price and specifications. The manufacturer was made to agree to a substantial price reduction, with the specifications agreed upon and stated in writing.

Supplier's Choice

Would the suppliers of the plane be justified in cutting corners and dropping some of the facilities specified in the contract and/or by providing parts or systems of an inferior quality?

The answer is a resounding no, and this is in the interests of both the parties and not merely of the Indian Air Force. In trade negotiations it is common for the supplier to quote a higher price so that the margin of profit is comfortable. When during negotiations he agrees to a lower price without the specifications being changed, it only means he is agreeing to a lower profit margin.

Good management by definition means sticking to the terms and conditions of the contract, and this includes quality. Even if this means a lower profit margin, it is in the interest of the supplier as much as it is in the interest of the party that placed the order that quality is not sacrificed.

Even though this is a large world, and there may be a number of suppliers of aircraft, or of printed greeting cards or other goods, there must be special reasons why a party orders goods from one supplier in preference to other suppliers. It may be quality, or a lower price, or convenience of delivery, or all of these.

Repeat Orders

Many or all of these considerations will continue to be valid in future. It is in the interest of the supplier that these considerations continue to prevail so that there are repeat orders and business continues to flow.

This is part of brand-building. If there is a deficiency in service on account of quality or time of delivery or any other reason, the brand suffers. Not only this, there will be no repeat orders and others who want to procure the same or similar goods/services will be wary of placing orders with the defaulting supplier.

Communication *Mantra* 5 of Management

All Parties must Gain: Management by definition means that all parties to a deal gain from it. If one party gains and the other loses, it is mismanagement.

The layman's understanding of a good bargain many a time is that he gains, whatever the gain or loss of the other party. The manager's definition of a good bargains is that both parties gain and no party loses.

Layman and Manager

If a layman becomes a Manager without internalizing the work culture of management, he may try to cut deals with his own gain in mind and unmindful of the other party's concerns. Typical of this is the attempt of the housewife to extract the lowest price from the vegetable seller, with the bonus of *dhaniya* and *mirchi* free of cost.

Good managers not only do not seek such deals, they studiously avoid them. Management involves the necessary ingredient of keeping the business flowing. An agreement in which you gain and the other party loses can at best be a one off deal. The result will be that either the other party will try to cut corners, for instance by compromising on quality in order to minimize his loss, or he will not enter a deal with you again. Frequently it will be both.

This means that business with that party will not flow again, and you lose the business partner you had selected after scouting the market. The best business practice is to select the best business partner and then to ensure that the partnership lasts so that business goes on uninterrupted.

Enduring Partnership

The best managers are, therefore, those who build up enduring business partnerships so that there is not only no interruption but business expands. This is the surest way to maximize gains from business. Remember that business is by definition entered into for continuing and maximum gains. No one enters business for minimal gains or occasional or continuing losses.

This applies as much to what in public relations are called "external publics" as to dealings with "internal publics".

Vendor's Case

An example of "external publics" is the supplier of particular parts to the Maruti factory for use in its cars. If the vender of parts does not make a profit, or incurs losses, he will either supply substandard parts or stop supplies. In both cases Maruti will have to restart the painful, expensive and time-consuming process of identifying a new vendor.

The most obvious example of "internal publics" is the workers of a factory. The smart Manager will try to give the best deal to his workers. This will ensure two things.

First, he will be able to insist on quality in production and high productivity. Secondly, he will have ensured that the best and most productive workers, painstakingly trained at considerable expense, do not try to migrate to other automobile manufacturing facilities.

It is possible to browbeat the workers, or a particular worker, into agreeing to a much lower wage than his experience and expertise warrant. This happens when the only alternative for the worker or group of workers is to lose the job. But this is a bad management practice which, most of the time, proves counter-productive.

Here are a few examples from my experience. In 1963, the *National Herald* daily of Lucknow lost nine sub-editors and reporters because of a personality clash with those managing the show. Junior reporters and sub-editors could be trained to replace them. But it would be expensive and time-consuming to train people to man senior positions.

A Coincidence

It so happened that almost at this time the *Leader* of Allahabad, one of the few other English language dailies in U.P., closed down. Rendered jobless, its journalists fanned out looking for jobs. Some came to Lucknow.

Among those who came to Lucknow was a Mr. R N Roy, a very senior and capable man with a lot of experience. He applied to the *Herald* for a job. I, as Chief sub-editor, was asked to give him a test.

I found him extremely competent and recommended his appointment. But as is the unintelligent practice employed by many managements, he was asked to specify the minimum salary at which he would agree to join. Jobless for many months and by now desperate, he mentioned an absurdly low figure, a sum the *Herald* was paying to learners.

The management was very happy that it would get a Senior sub-editor at a junior man's salary. But News Editor Charlie Baptista in his wisdom rejected the salary specified.

"If he is as good as you say," Baptista told me, "he must be given a salary commensurate with his experience and expertise." I was advised to tell him to put in a substitute application asking for a sum commensurate with his expertise.

Desperate Situation

I told Mr. Roy of the requirement. "But what if they reject the higher figure as too high?" he told me frankly. "I am desperate".

He was assured that his demand for a higher salary would not be rejected. Mr. Roy put in a substitute application, was appointed, and continued with the paper until retirement.

Here is another story, this one relating to what happened when a short-sighted Manager tried to pin down good workers to a low salary and a lower position than they deserved. In 1984 I came down from the *Statesman* in Delhi and joined the *Pioneer*, another Lucknow daily, as Deputy Editor, rising to be its Editor in a year.

Promotion Refused

There were in the *Pioneer* those days two very senior sub-editors taking charge of editions pretty competently.

Taking charge of editions is usually done by a Chief sub-editor, but the General Manager, unintelligently thinking he could extract the Chief sub-editor's work while paying a sub-editor's salary to them, refused them promotion to the higher grade.

About this time, the *Times of India* (of Bombay and Delhi) started an edition in Lucknow. It looked around for local journalists and found these two bright young men doing the Chief Sub's job on a sub-editor's salary. It gave them a test, found them competent as Chief Subs and took them on. They formed the backbone of the *Times of India's* Lucknow edition.

The *Pioneer* lost them because its management thought it was smart to extract the Chief Sub's work while paying the sub-editor's salary!

The two young men, now not all that young, are Atul Chandra and Ratan Mani Lal. On a private visit to Lucknow in 2005, I found Atul enthroned as the Resident Editor of the *Times of India*. Ratan I found to be the Director of a thriving communication institute in Lucknow which had plans to open a branch in NOIDA.

SUMMING UP

1. All transactions involve more than one party. Hence, it is mandatory to respond to all business messages, whether written, oral or conveyed in any other way.

2. Communication should be as specific as possible leaving no doubt or ambiguity.

3. Don't keep business partner guessing. Don't say "as soon as possible", say "on October 18" or "at 10 a.m. on October 18".

4. Specifications of quality, quantity, etc., of contract are sacrosanct, even if price has been scaled down during negotiations.

5. Build up trust that nothing agreed upon will be departed from. This is necessary for brand-building.

Self-Check Exercises

1. A supplier quotes a price for a contract for a certain quantity of work of a specific quality. During negotiations he scales down the price. Can he scale down quantity and quality? It not, why not? Answer in the space provided.

   (Space for answer)

2. A supplier of wall tiles writes to the party that ordered it: "The tiles will be made ready as soon as we get the raw material." Is this a good business communication? Give reasons for your answer.

   (Space for answer)

3. Party X writes to Supplier Y to supply 10,000 glazed tiles. Supplier Y replies that the 10,000 tiles ordered will be ready on October 15 at 10 a.m. Is this the proper and complete answer?

   (Space for answer)

15

Some Norms for the Usage of Words and Expressions

Each one who communicates in English is supposed to know all the rules of grammar and the spellings. Each one also believes he knows the correct usage of the words and expressions he uses, but I wish this were so.

The sequence in which words and expressions are used in a sentence makes a difference. When I was in Dhenkanal, Orissa, running a post-graduate course in English language journalism for the Indian Institute of Mass Communication, one of the English language slogans painted on walls in the town read, "K P Singh Deo, Long Live, Long Live."

Whoever got the slogan painted all over the town to eulogize the local M.P. obviously thought in Oriya or Hindi, in which language one would say, "K P Singh Deo Amar Rahein, Amar Rahein, Amar Rahein", and then translated it into English. Had the slogan been thought in English, it would have read, "Long Live K P Singh Deo."

In the journalism class also, though the students had come through an all-India admission test, some children still thought it was all right to formulate the sentence in Oriya , Hindi, Bangla or Malayalam and translate it into English. How I made the students get into the habit of formulating the sentence in English if they were writing in that language, and what a herculean effort it took, is to be found in my forthcoming book *Our Dhenkanal Children*.

Sequence of Words

It is necessary to realize that the sequence of words to say the same thing is liable to differ from language to language. In English, a change in the placing of a word in the sentence frequently changes the meaning drastically. "Ram alone came to school" means Ram was the only one to come to school. But "Ram came alone to school"? It means Ram was not accompanied on the way to school.

Change the placing of the word "alonc" again. Let the sentence read, "Ram came to school alone." It would mean that Ram's only destination was school. He had no other errand to run, or to see the doctor, or to visit a friend.

When, however, you say "Ram alone *went* to school" the focus shifts to the place of departure, that is the house, building or *mohalla* from where he came, and not the place of arrival, that is the school. It implies that of the many children in the house/building /*mohalla*, only Ram went to school.

If you are telling the story of the Ram-Ravana conflict, you can end up by saying, "Ram killed Ravana." Note the juxtaposition of words: subject followed by verb followed by object. But literally translated into Hindi, it will read, *Ram ne maara Ravana ko*." This is grammatically not incorrect but inappropriate if you are stating the culmination of the conflict in plain prose. In poetry, however, it may be permissible if the aim is either to set the meter right or to make the last word "ko" rhyme with a similar last word in a preceding or following line.

'And' and 'Or'

A sentence in a newspaper write-up on the eve of the third India-West Indies ODI reads: "Sreesanth, or if he is rested Munaf Patel, are to share the new ball with Irfan Pathan, who is a certainty." What is right in this sentence and what is wrong? If it is either Sreesanth or Munaf Patel, it is only one man, not both. So it should be "Sreesanth, or if he is rested Munaf Patel, is to share the new ball with Irfan Pathan, who is a certainty".

Where more than one name is mentioned, the writer may get the impression that all those mentioned together form the subject. But if there is an *or* between two names, it is either the one or the other, so it is singular. But where there is an *and* joining two or more names, they are many persons and hence plural. So "Sreesanth and Munaf Patel are to open the bowling" is perfectly all right.

Reuter's Gaffe

Here is another example – and this aberration took place during British rule when the English language was supposed to reign supreme. It was 1944 and Allied forces had landed in Normandy, France, to open the second front against Hitler's Germany (the first front was in Eastern Europe where Soviet forces were fighting Germany). A despatch by Reuter, the British news agency, read: *"The Allied army, consisting of British, American and Candidan contigents, are equipped with one thousand tanks and 390 guns, and are protected by British and American warplanes."*

True, the Allied army consisted of contigents from three countries, but it was still one army. Therefore, it should have been treated as singular, not plural.

The Trick

If there is any doubt whether it is singular or plural, the trick is to take out the parenthetical clause and see how it reads. If the reporter filing the news story, or the sub-editor who okayed it for transmission, had taken this precaution, he would have realized that it was one army. The parenthetical clause is "consisting of British, American and Canadian contigents." If we take it out, the sentence reads: "The Allied army...are", which is silly. An army always *is*, it can never be *are*.

Business Communication

Here is a similar communication, this time from a business house, which has got tripped.

> *The plant, including three boilers, three pumps and a lot of ancillaries including heaters, circuit breakers and cooling towers, are to be installed and tested by December 30.*

True, there are three boilers, three pumps and a host of other equipment. But they form part of a single plant since the sentence uses the word *including*. Hence *are* is wrong here. It should be *is*.

Two Ways

Here are two ways of saying the same thing, one in singular and the other in plural :

1. Dravid's team, consisting of 14 players and three officials, is proceeding to St. Kitts today for the third ODI.

2. Dravid and his team, consisting of 14 players and three officials, are proceeding to St. Kitts today for the third ODI.

The difference is that the first talks of Dravid's team, which is one even though consisting of many players and officials, while the second talks of Dravid *and* his team, which makes it two entities. One entity is Dravid and the other is his team. Hence the verb has to be *are*.

MBAs and Non-MBAs

It can be argued that business communication is all about plants, machinery, teams of workers, etc., and the verb does not matter to the seasoned business man.

This looks true to an extent. You are not addressing a Professor of English, only cricket enthusiasts who care for the game or business men who care for business and profit and not about the verb you use.

But supposing they understand the meanings of words, too, and know which verb to use where? It will jar them, and quite unnecessarily.

Ask all the successful men in society, and each one will tell you he will bargain hard, but will simultaneously go out of his way to be courteous. Amitabh Bachchan is known never to rub his fans or fellow workers (even clapper boys) on the wrong side. But he makes hard bargains where business matters are concerned.

Throughout the *Kaun Banega Crorepati* episides he flaunted a beard. The reason was that the next films he was about to appear in required him to be bearded. It was a concession to the demand of the film. But ask the film-maker whether he was able to wheedle a concession in business terms out of him, and the answer will be a flat "no".

Cost of Quality

No compromise: Take Dhirubhai Ambani, H P Nanda and Raunaq Singh. Each of them founded a business empire anyone would be proud of. All have been not only courteous to a fault but yielding in everything – everything except business matters. In business matters one has to take a stand after taking into account all the inputs, like cost of raw materials, cost of transportation, taxes, the profit margin, etc. After all, one has to maintain quality and stick to the time schedule. How does one maintain quality and stick to the schedule if he makes compromises on inputs?

There is something called image, which must be created and maintained and must never be allowed to be sullied. This image works as much for the business man as his work itself. This has been discussed in an earlier chapter.

To revert to the language of communication, the language one uses in written communication is as important for business as, and probably more important than, the language he uses orally. We live in times when business men realize that mastery of the language one uses is as important as mastering the input-output ratio. That is why there is such a rush for admission to business courses.

In your father's time, and most certainly in my father's, there were no MBAs. Young people learnt the tricks of the trade, including monkey tricks, on the job, either from the family elder or as apprentices in other people's businesses.

No Verbosity

The secrets of today's business communication are correctness, accuracy, clarity and, invariably, courtesy even when one is saying "no". The old world verbosity of pre-war days is out.

Before the war, the British rulers had taught us to say, perhaps to make us aware of the reality, "I beg to remain, Sir, your most obedient servant" at the end of a letter. Never even in one's sleep should one use this expression now. "Yours sincerely" is good enough to assure the other party of one's earnestness for the business transaction.

Also out are beginnings like "we beg to acknowledge receipt of...", "In compliance with your esteemed order of.....", "We beg to inform you....", etc. Don't beg, just inform.

These are the "don'ts". The most important of the "do's is to establish personal rapport even in written communication. Say, for instance, "As instructed in your letter of June 25, 2002, we confirm that the 25 tarpaulins ordered will be delivered at your factory at 2 Dwarkadas Road on August 2". Best of all will, of course, be to specify even the time apart from the date. For instance, "The 25 tarpaulines will be delivered at your factory at 2 Dwarkadas Road at 12 noon on August 2."

This will relieve him of every anxiety and, additionally, enable him to depute someone to receive the consignment.

Verbiage

Unnecessary verbiage, while meant to please, only irritates the other party. Shun verbiage like "thanking you in anticipation", "assuring you of our best services at all times..." "at your earliest convenience", "in due course of time" and "trusting to be favoured with further orders." If you have done good service this time, further orders are bound to come. You don't need to give an assurance of your best services. Give them the best of services and let them evaluate what they have got and appreciate it. If you have not given the best service, they will only sneer at your assurance.

'As Soon As Possible'

Vagueness in communication is the enemy of business management. "The consignment will be delivered as soon as possible" is meaningless because nothing can be delivered until it is possible. It is officialese and is best buried in official jargon. If you can specify the date, time and place of delivery, nothing like it. If it is contingent on something happening, specify it and give them the time frame as accurately as you can.

For instance, "our consignment of special steel has reached Bombay port from the manufacturers in the USA. Our effort is bring it to Delhi by May 30. It will take 72 hours for us to manufacture the 25 implements you have ordered and within six hours of manufacture they will be delivered to you. We will inform you the moment the special steel is received at our foundry from Bombay port."

Ambiguity or vagueness in business dealings is by far the biggest of irritants and can sour the most carefully cultivated relationship because it thwarts all attempts by the other party of fulfil its commitments.

SUMMING UP

The placing of a word or an expression in a sentence determines the message the sentence gives. *Ram alone came to school* means that Ram was the only one who came. *Ram came alone to school* means that he came to school unaccompanied by anyone.

Ram killed Ravana keeps the focus on Ram's deed. *Ravana was killed by Ram* shifts the focus to Ravana's fate.

"Ram, Lakshman and Sita were eating together" is the right way to put it. "Ram, Lakshman or Sita were eating" is wrong, since only one of them was eating.

Using unnecessary words disperses the focus from the message one wants to convey. Expressions like "assuring you of our best services at all times" is an example.

Self-Check Exercises

1. Write the following in the correct from :

(a) India, along with South Africa and Sri Lanka, are to participate in a triangular ODI Series.

(Space for answer)

(b) India, South Africa and Sri Lanka is to participate in a triangular ODI series.

(Space for answer)

2. X receives an order for five lakh glazed yellow bathroom tiles. He replies : "Many thanks for your patronage in placing an order for the commodity you need in your letter of even date."

   Find fault with this reply, giving reasons.

   (Space for answer)

PART II

BUSINESS COMMUNICATION

16

Different Kinds of Business Communication

Business is the work one does, and to work one has to communicate. The aims of communication, however, vary. One kind of work involves personal or family goals. It requires interpersonal business communication. For instance, the woman of the house may ask one to bring a litre of milk. The man goes to the market, tenders the money and obtains milk.

Alternatively, if he is writing a letter to be dropped in the letterbox before the postman arrives for the clearance, it may be agreed that he would write the letter and post it before bringing the milk. There has been interpersonal communication between the man and the woman to achieve common family goals.

There is, then, official-business, business communication. Here also the communication takes place but the goals of the two parties may differ. A citizen goes to an office to get his work done. Ideally, the goal of the citizen and the goal of the official approached should converge. For, the citizen has come to get work done, and the official has come to office to do it.

But frequently this convergence does not take place. For, the official is bound by procedure. His primary goal is to follow the prescribed procedure, and often the perception is that the work he has come to do will be only the outcome of the procedure.

The citizen has two choices, either to argue his case and convince the official, in which case the work is done, or to agree to abide by the procedure in which case it takes time, sometimes hours and sometimes days or months.

Here I am not talking of deliberate stalling, harassment or corruption. If an official wants a bribe or to settle personal scores, that is another matter entirely and out of the scope of this discussion. The purpose is to stress that official-business business communication takes a path all its own because officials have to give primary importance to procedure. The goal of accomplishing the goal is subject to the prescribed procedure.

UTI Case

If former UTI Chairman Subramaniam and Executive Directors M M Kapur and S K Basu were indicted in 2003, the primary reason was not that they had bought Cyberspace Infosys shares for UTI worth Rs. 32 crores. Even the price paid might be excused, exorbitant as it was.

Their major fault was that they overruled the recommendation of the UTI research team which had advised against the deal. The proper procedure was to either accept the recommendation of the research team which is an expert body or, if they did not, to state what clinching information made them go through the deal against expert advice.

If they had cited the piece of information and it had turned out to be wrong, they could at the most be accused of lacking in judgment and using their discretion unwisely, which is not a crime though it can be censured. According to legal experts cited in newspaper reports, when Subramaniam claimed at the time of arrest that he had been under pressure and received telephone calls from various sources which made him buy the shares, it was evident that he had not followed the proper procedure and therefore his conduct was unlawful.

Here is an example of official-business business communication from my experience. In 1968 when my second child was born my wife had to stay in the private ward of the Lady Hardinge Medical College Hospital in Delhi for more than a month because of certain medical complications. She was under the treatment of a team headed by Professor Pinto de Rozairo, Head of the Department of Gynaecology, and consisting of Dr. Arora, Associate Professor in the department, and half a dozen doctors junior to them.

At the end of it I was given a discharge slip and a receipt for the money charged from me. I deposited it with the *Statesman*, the organization I was serving, for reimbursement of the expenditure.

The Objection

The official who received my application raised the objection that for reimbursement the bill had to be signed and certified by a "registered medical practitioner". That was the procedure.

No matter how much I protested that it had been signed by the professor who produced dozens of "registered medical practitioners" every year, the Accounts Department remained unmoved. It was even suggested that if the professor and the associate professor were difficult to access, I could get the document counter-signed by a junior doctor, but his or her registration number had to be there.

It so happens that the junior doctors, though registered medical practitioners, were – and always are in a medical college – still learners whose main job was to learn from what all the professors did, to administer the intraveinous injections prescribed and even to note down the prescription dictated by the senior.

To ask or expect them to countersign a document signed by the professor would be insulting to the senior and would never be done by the junior. It was ultimately the intervention of the *Statesman's* Managing Director, who waived the requirement, which enabled me to get the reimbursement.

A Contrast

In contrast with the interpersonal business and official-business business communication, there is something called business- business business communication. The business man's goal is to get a certain work done. While the prescribed procedure should be followed, if there are hurdles there can be alternative procedures which can cross these hurdles.

A business man goes to a firm and wants to buy one lakh glazed tiles of a certain quality, size and colour, deliverable in a week. If the person receiving the order is an official or has the attitude of an official, he would think of the prescribed procedure under which all orders for tiles have to be made a month before delivery.

If, on the other hand, he is also a business man or has the business man's attitude, he would immediately consider how to bypass this hurdle if it cannot be crossed. Are there such tiles in stock? If yes, his response to the order will be positive. If they are not in stock, can they be manufactured in a week? Surely the standing rule that orders have to be placed a month before delivery cannot mean that delivery should be stalled even if the order can be executed earlier.

If there are earlier orders for tiles being executed, can these earlier orders be put on hold? They can be put on hold if the earlier buyer wanted the tiles only after six weeks but they are being manufactured and stored for delivery at the appropriate time. If all this fails, can one as a last resort buy tiles form another manufacturer at a discount in order to execute the order?

In 1958 I was Editor of the *People* weekly in Lucknow. Being still unmarried, I had taken on rent a house with two other single men, Pankaj and Hajela. One Saturday evening, as I was about to call it a day at 6 p.m., Pankaj walked in with the request to compose and print several thousand copies of half a dozen forms his office wanted by Monday.

On to Rama Press

Our office normally did not do job work because it had its hands full composing and printing the *People* and its Hindi sister publication *Janmat*. I would still have obliged Pankaj but all the press workers had gone home and would report back for work only on Monday morning. What to do?

I consulted our all-knowing handyman Mangal who had lived in the area since birth and knew about all the composing and printing facilities in the area. Sure enough, he suggested that we go to Rama Press which was a kilometer away.

At Rama Press, the proprietor wanted extra payment since it was a rush job and would require overtime work all night. But where was the paper? The paper shops were also closed on Sunday.

Pankaj made a few phone calls and reported that his boss had agreed to the terms. The paper would be at Rama Press on Sunday morning. The printed forms were delivered on Monday.

Had I been an official, I would have said sorry, since our press was closed and the men had gone home. But we found a way out by going to a press which worked on Sunday and which undertook to do the work for a small extra charge. Such is business-business business communication.

SUMMING UP

Business communication is necessary to get work done. In interpersonal business communication, the goal is usually the achievement of personal or family goals.

In official-business business communication, the focus of the official side is on following prescribed procedures. Departures from them are not allowed. The achievement of the goal or goals is an outcome of following the prescribed procedure.

In business-business business communication, the goal of both parties is the same, and both strive for its achievement. If the prescribed procedure has hurdles, attempts are made to cross them or alternative procedures are explored.

In interpersonal business communication, the parties are separate individuals, frequently members of a family or community.

In official-official business communication, one of the parties is either an official following set procedures, or a non-official similarly obsessed with procedure.

In business-business business communication, both parties have a business like attitude and pursue whichever path leads to the achievement of the goal.

Self-Check Exercises

1. You go to a business man to buy one lakh yellow tiles deliverable in one week. His factory is manufacturing sky blue tiles and the process will be over in two days. After that he will execute your order, but by the seventh day from now he will be able to deliver 70,000 yellow tiles. The remaining 30,000 he promises to deliver in two more days without charging extra cartage. What will you decide? Give reasons.

   (Leave enough space for answer)

2. It is nowadays said that business is not the Government's business. What reasons are cited for this comment?

(Leave enough space for answer)

17 Production, Progress and Other Reports

Management involves a lot of writing of reports. If you are running an organization, or a project of an organization, you will have to make periodical production reports maybe orally but mostly in writing. If it is a new project, you will have to make periodical progress reports. These are also called status reports, that is, what is the status of the project.

Production reports may be formal or informal, but in the interest of the organization as well as oneself it is desirable to make formal reports. It is also desirable, indeed necessary, to keep a file of successive production reports. One himself needs to review the ongoing situation periodically in order to better plan for the future. This is apart from the file which the Production Director would have to keep.

(A) Production Report

There has over time developed a set format for periodical production reports. First the date is given, then the person to whom the report is being made, then the person from whom it comes, then the subject. After this comes the content of the report. In order that the situation is clear at a glance, a table format is used. Table-1 is a sample format.

This is a sample of the production report. For any given enterprise a series of periodical production reports, filed at regular intervals, will be necessary to enable the organization

Table 1. – Production Report

Date	August 1, 2006
To	Production Manager
From	Plant Manager
Subject	Production of tiles July 2006

	July	**June**	**Increase**
No. of tiles produced	30,000	22,500	7,500

It has been possible to increase production by 33 per cent by removing the bottlenecks in the process. The successive operations which were earlier carried out in different locations have been relocated so that immediately after one operation is completed the next operation starts with only a split second of time lag.

Plans for August

It is planned to consolidate the new procedure adopted so that there is no slippage. The plant is able to meet the current demand in full in time. If Marketing Department is able to increase the bookings by a minimum of 5,000 tiles, one more production unit will have to be added to the existing four units.

to keep track of work and, when necessary, to change the working and production schedule. When necessary the management may ask for mid-term production reports, for instance when a new urgent order is received, or when the order being executed is modified by the client midway through.

For instance, when 60,000 tiles have been produced the client may decide that instead of 40,000 more yellow tiles it needs 60,000 more tiles but in sky blue, not yellow.

Omnibus Term

"Production report" is an omnibus term which encompasses not only the process of production but sales and other productive activities. A company's sales manager for a particular territory would at regular intervals report the sales for particular periods to the Sales Director. If there is no marketing department, which means the sales department doubles up as the marketing department booking sales and contacting potential clients, its report would indicate how well the existing clients have been serviced and how many potential clients were contacted and how many of them placed orders and became actual clients.

In all cases, however, the report is called "production report" unless a particular company has decided to give it the name " sales report" or any other name. The reason is that the word "production" is deemed to mean the production of value, not of tiles or cloth or any particular commodity.

Table 2. – Production Report

Date	August 1, 2006
To	Marketing Director
From	Marketing Manager, Ghaziabad
Subject	Marketing of tiles July 2006

Sales of tiles increased in July 2001 by 10% over the previous month by virtue of additional bookings from existing clients. As a result of a vigorous marketing drive 5 new clients placed orders for a total of 20,000 tiles to be supplied in September.

Established Clients

Orders booked from existing clients – 1,10,000 numbers. This is 10% higher than June's orders totalling 100,000.

New Clients

Number of prospective clients approached	40
New clients enlisted out of 40 approached	5

Orders booked for September from new clients 20,000 numbers

The marketing manager for a particular territory will make similar production reports, but with a difference. For his job is not only to book orders from existing clients but to try to enlist new clients. Table-2 is a sample of the production report the marketing manager for a particular territory will make to his Marketing Director.

(B) Progress Report

The progress report is the report of the executing unit on the establishment of a new unit of the organization. It may be a new production unit or a marketing unit. A particular manufacturer of tiles with its production facility in Alwar, Rajasthan, had divided its marketing area into five territories. One of the territories was based on Delhi and covered not only Delhi but the whole of the former district of Ghaziabad. With growth in sales in both Delhi and Ghaziabad and, further, with the bifurcation of the Ghaziabad district into Ghaziabad and Gautam Budh Nagar, it decides to separate marketing operations in these two western U.P. districts from its work in Delhi A separate office is established in Ghaziabad town to undertake operations in these two districts.

This is decided in July 2006 and the Ghaziabad office is established on August 1. It is supposed to take over operations in the districts of Ghaziabad and Gautam Budh Nagar.

On August 1 the marketing manager for the newly carved territory takes charge. He is required to send weekly progress reports to the Marketing Director in Alwar until the process of the establishment of the new territorial marketing unit is complete. Table-3 is a sample of his progress report filed for the second week.

(C) Non- Routine Reports

Production Report and Progress Report are considered routine reports. In the case of the production of a manufacturing or marketing unit, reports have routinely to

Table 3. – Progress Report

Date	August 14, 2006
To	Marketing Director, Alwar
From	Marketing Manager, Ghaziabad
Subject	Establishment of Ghaziabad Marketing Territory

Marketing Manager, Ghaziabad, took over operations in the newly created territory from Marketing Manager, Delhi, on August 1. By August 7 all the marketing personnel in the territory had started reporting to Marketing Manager, Ghaziabad. Bookings achieved during this week were of the same level as during the previous week.

Bookings during the week ended August 14 were 20% higher than during the previous week.

Problems Encountered

Since only one of the three telephones ordered had been installed up to August 1, sales personnel found it difficult to contact the Ghaziabad office. The remaining two telephones were installed on August 8 and sales personnel found it easier to contact the Ghaziabad office.

Target For Remainder of Job

The objective of establishing a new territorial office in Ghaziabad was to increase sales in the territory by 50% per month. Since only a 20% increase was achieved up to August 14, the target for the two weeks ending August 31 is to achieve the marketing target by raising booking of orders by 30 percentage points over July.

be made at intervals, or sometimes when required by the Production Director or Marketing Director.

In the case of a new unit being set up, Progress Report has to be made at intervals until the process of setting it up is completed. In both cases the man to whom the report has to be made is usually a technical specialist.

This does not always mean that he is an engineer. In the case of physical production by working on and moulding raw materials into the finished product, it has of necessity to be an engineer. But in the case of marketing, he is a specialist in sales and in that sense a technical specialist.

Major Consumer

Suppose our company sets up a separate sales office in Ghaziabad. Earlier the area was part of what is called the Delhi Territory. But in the past two decades, Ghaziabad has been developing into a major consumer of glazed tiles, something that it was not earlier. This is because Delhi became too crowded with commercial concerns and middle class residents.

Why middle class? Because only middle class households use glazed titles in their houses on any significant scale. Peasants, laboureres, construction workers, even plumbers do not use glazed tiles in their homes to any significant extent.

When I was building my house in Delhi, there were four labour contractors – masonry, plumbing, electrical and woodwork. Sabir was the plumbing contractor. He advised me and executed the laying of sewer and water pipelines, the lavatories, the bathrooms, the manholes, etc. His role came only in fits and starts. So at stages at which he had to play a role he had to be called.

Usually I sent a message, but sometimes had to go myself. I found that his dwelling in the Kutcha Tihar village had no bathroom or lavatory of the type we know because there were no sewer or water pipelines to the village. Yet he advised me on where to use glazed tiles, up to what height, etc.

Now, with Ghaziabad which earlier included NOIDA, and Gurgaon developing into locations for commercial establishments and middle class dwellings, the consumption of glazed tiles has gone up dramatically. So the company decided to make the area a separate marketing territory controlled by a marketing office in Ghaziabad town.

Why is the work of the sales office monitored through Production Reports? Because, the amount of sales is classed as the production of that office. A rise or fall in sales is classed as a rise or fall in production.

There are, then, situations in which a report has to be made by a unit or team or individual given a job *ad hoc*. Such reports are called non-routine reports. An example of a non-routine report is one made by a team entrusted the job, for instance, of finding out the housewives' preference between carton-packed and bag-packed spices. The team given the job has first to decide where and how to contact housewives.

The team may decide to send its personnel to make a house-to-house survey. In this method men or women of the team go to individual houses and ask housewives the relevant questions. The team has to ensure that the same questions are asked from each housewife in the same order and the answers are noted down. Usually even the answers are preset. For instance –

Question : Do you want ground turmeric in cartons or bags of 100 gm?

Answer : (a) bags
(b) cartons
(c) whichever is cheaper
(d) no opinion

The person goes from house to house and poses the question to each housewife in the way it is worded, and asks her to choose between the four answers provided. These reports are then collected, collated and analyzed, which in turn enables the company to choose its pattern of production.

(D) Interview Report

House-to-house survey is but one way to find out whether housewives want spices packed in cartons or bags. Another way, and perhaps a better way for this purpose, is to post personnel at grocery stores to ask these questions of those who come to buy things. A great advantage is that the person who goes to a store to buy things has only the grocery on her mind.

The housewife accosted at home may be worried about the milk boiling over, or the maid being late, or preparing breakfast in time for the children going to school. She will have to take the mind off the job in hand to attend to the question. While how to package spices is uppermost in the company's mind, the housewife at home would have to switch over to this issue which may look trivial to her compared to what she is doing.

A way frequently used in more developed countries is to distribute a questionnaire, then to collect the filled form some hours later. In India this method has been found to be less successful, especially on issues as mundane as packaging spices. Besides, literacy is low in India, and women are specially disinclined to take up the pen to answer questions. They would any day prefer to answer verbally.

In whichever way we approach the prospective consumer, however, post-questioning the procedure is the same. One totals separately the number of housewives who want cartons and those who want bags. A third column carries the numbers who want whichever – the carton or the bag – is less costly to the consumer, and the fourth carries the number of those who don't care whether it is the carton or the bag. The fourth column includes also those who don't reply, the assumption being that it does not matter enough to them. The data are to be tabulated as in Table-4:

But the C-3, block is only a small part of the Janakpuri market where the company's spices are sold. They are also

Table 4. – Interview Report

Date	
To	
From	
Subject	Finding out whether consumers prefer spices packed in cartons or bags.
Subject	Customers questioned at 3 groceries in C-3 block, Janakpuri
Households Covered	300

Preference for cartons	50
Preference for bags	60
Whichever less costly to consumer	120
No reply	70

Result: 120/300 prefer whichever is less costly to consumer
70/300 no reply
60/300 prefer bags
50/300 prefer cartons

Analysis: Since bags will be less costly than cartons to the customer, 120+60 = 180/300 can be taken to prefer bags.

Recommendation: 180/300, that is 60%, prefer bags. Hence packing of spices in bags recommended.

sold in less affluent areas, for instance the Possangipur village which is part of Janakpuri, as well as A-l block where more affluent people live in huge bungalows. The decision of the company will depend on the following factors:

(A) Whether the company is new to Janakpuri, and if it wants to target the more affluent but fewer families of Janakpuri or whether it wants larger volumes for which it will have to target the less affluent pockets like C-3 and C-5 blocks.

(B) Whether it is already popular in the less affluent pockets and wants to penetrate the affluent families, or vice versa.

(C) Whether it is at present selling spices in cartons alone, or in bags alone, or in both.

If it is only angling for the convenience of one mode of packaging, it may decide to opt for bags given that 60% of the households surveyed want bags and hope to persuade the rest to fall in line. If it is not a this-or-that situation, the company may decide to send only cartons to the more affluent areas and only bags to the less affluent.

The collection of data through interviews is thus crucial. Whether the decision turns out to be advantageous to the company or disadvantageous will depend on the accuracy of the data, the size of the sample selected and how representative that sample is. The interview report can thus be crucial to the company's spice business.

(E) Feasibility Report

Feasibility Report is another important kind of non-routine report. This is usually commissioned when an organization wants to ascertain things like –

1. Whether the introduction of a particular service or commodity in a particular area will be useful, and if yes how useful, to the organization. For instance whether pizzas will be sufficiently popular in Janakpuri for an outlet to be opened.
2. Whether a change in the manner of delivery of a commodity or service will be successful. For instance, whether banks should continue to have an off day once a week or whether opening on the seventh day of the week will yield sufficient gain to be resorted to.

Conversely, whether it will make a sufficient difference to be a perceptible disadvantage if the Bank, which works seven days a week, is closed one day a week. In such cases, an interview-based and a questionnaire-based survey will be equally useful because all the bank customers are expected to be comfortable with the written message.

Two Methods

If it is the case of introducing pizzas, personnel can be sent on a house-to-house survey, or posted outside existing restaurants to elicit the opinion of patrons. The questions have to be definite and will depend on what the survey aims to find out. Here are some sample questions:

(1) How many times a month do you go outside Janakpuri to eat pizzas?

(2) If a pizza joint is opened in the colony how many times a month do you think you would visit it?

(3) Would you go alone or would you take the whole family along?

(4) If pizzas of satisfactory taste, varieties and standard are available at an existing restaurant, whether you would want to opt for pizza (a) every time you visit the restaurant (b) half the times (c) never at all (d) can't say.

The analysis and recommendation will follow the pattern etched in the case of other interview-based reports. Once again, the way the questions are framed and the thoroughness and accuracy of the analysis and recommendation will be vital.

Here is another kind of feasibility report. Your company wants to enter a market, or it wants to start a new line of production, that is, something it has not been producing before. This desire may be triggered off by the fact that another company producing that product is highly successful and profitable.

A second situation which may act as a trigger is the fact that society finds it messy to carry out an operation as it has been doing and wants a simpler, less time consuming and less laborious and less costly way, and such a way has been found.

A third trigger can be the desire for value addition. That is, you find that a product superior to that which is in use can be produced. Example: first black and white photocopying and then colour. A fourth can be fashion – a cosmetic change to make things look, or feel, better.

Dalda's Case

An example of fashion is the start of the production in India of hydrogenated vegetable oil. Do you know what it means? It simply means a change in appearance with the content remaining more or less the same. Here is an example in the Indian context.

Before World War II, India in common with the rest of this sub-continent had two clear cut cooking mediums. One was ghee, which is now called *desi ghee* (why the word *desi* has been added will be explained later in this narrative). The other was edible oil extracted from oilseeds and other organic products. Ghee was prepared from milk, predominantly cow's or buffalo's.

In Europe, the Americas and much of Africa and perhaps in many parts of Asia *ghee* was not used. Instead they used other forms of animals fat and butter. *Ghee*, the British say, is clarified butter.

Ghee was the elite's cooking medium in undivided India. Only those who could afford used it, which meant only the elite of society. The rest used oil extracted from vegetation - coconut, peanuts, mustard, til, etc. The elite used cooking oil only for special dishes in which the oil's flavour was preferred to *ghee's*.

For instance, pakoras were mostly fried in mustard oil in North India. Bengalis preferred to fry their fish in mustard oil. In coastal areas where coconuts are grown in abundance, most of the cooking was in coconut oil except in dishes where *ghee* was preferred.

The plebeians in all of India had no choice but to use oil because *ghee* was several times costlier. To be seen using cooking oil in place of *ghee* was, therefore, considered a sure sign that one did not belong to the elite of society.

Vanaspati Ghee

Came the war and everything became costlier, including *ghee*. But along with the war also came the technology of converting edible oil into something which looked like *ghee*. The same white colour was there and the liquid was turned by hydrogenation into a *ghee*-like solid. Only the *ghee* flavour was missing. The substance was later called *vanaspati* (or vegetation) *ghee*, to distinguish it from *ghee* extracted out of milk.

The first name by which it became popular was Dalda. This is because it was first introduced in India by the multinational Level Brothers (parent of today's Hindustan Lever) under the generic name Dalda. I remember hearing about it for the first time in a 10-second commercial shown before the Hindi film *Khazanchi* which my parents had taken me and my siblings to see in a cinema hall. The commercial showed a tin of Dalda around which was dancing a character singing *Yehi Dalda, Yehi Dalda*. Later Dalda was brought to our house and food was cooked in it.

In contrast with the elite, the non-elite classes did all their cooking in whichever edible oil was available at low cost in the area. In the south and in the coastal regions where coconuts grow aplenty the commonest cooking medium was coconut oil.

In the north, however, coconut or its oil had to be brought all the way from the coasts and so it was costly compared to oilseeds like mustard which are locally grown and are cheap. Consequently, most of the cooking among the non-elite classes in this area was done in mustard, or *alsi* or *teesi* oil which is cheaper even than mustard.

Similarity to Ghee

The advent of Dalda as it was commonly and universally known in the initial years changed this. It looked like *ghee* and did not smell like oil, and the cost was only marginally higher than the cost of edible oil and substantially lower than *ghee's*. The non-elite classes therefore took to it in a big way in order to move one rung higher on the social ladder.

There were four clear advantages. First, it did not have the flavour which each edible oil has peculiar to itself and which told everybody within sniffing distance that the family was not using *ghee* but oil, downgrading it in social esteem.

Though Dalda did not have the pleasant flavour peculiar to *ghee*, it was all right since when food was being cooked in it no one would know from the smell that anything as downmarket as cooking oil was being used.

Second Dalda looked deceptively like ghee. These two qualities enticed people into using Dalda while pretending that they used *ghee*. One could always use a tiny bit of *ghee* to give that peculiar pleasant whiff to the food.

The third reason was that Dalda was priced a fraction of *ghee's* price and only marginally higher than oil's. The marginal increase in cost was necessary to absorb the small cost of hydrogenation.

I have seen people buying Dalda loose in their ghee containers to mislead onlookers. It was also very common for people to buy Dalda in the original container and cover it with a towel or hide it inside a bag while taking it home lest anyone see they are carrying home Dalda.

Classic Example

This is how good old *ghee* came to be christened *desi* (indigenous) *ghee* to distinguished it from Dalda which was called *vilayati* or foreign *ghee*.

We were discussing how fashion comes to trigger a new line of production distinct from and unrelated to a company's original product. Vanaspati, as Dalda came to be rightly called when companies other than Levers started producing it, is a classic example of this.

A very large number of companies whose line of business had nothing to do with food started producing it because the technology was very simple and required a very small investment and the profit was substantial and assured, given the large number of consumers who aspired to climb one step higher on the social ladder.

Buy edible oil at price X, convert it to vanaspati costing X+l, and sell it at price X+3 or X+4. Lever's Dalda was soon followed by Rath, manufactured by Delhi Cloth Mills (DCM) which was a cloth manufacturer and had never made any food item before. Other vanaspati manufacturers followed, people whose main line of production was something else but who didn't want to miss the opportunity to make the fast buck through a little of investment and the minimum of effort.

The emergence of vanaspati gives an idea of what a Feasibility Report would contain. It includes inquiries and findings in four key areas:

1. ***The Market:*** How big is the market? That is, how much is consumed in a given area per unit of time, say one year. The survey of the size of the market includes a survey of competitors who are making and selling the product under a different brand name.

   Is there enough production to feed the market? Is the production deficient leading to a scarcity? Or is there more production than demand leading to intense competition? Can our company make the product at the same cost as the competitors, at a lower cost, or at a higher cost?

2. ***The Input:*** Are the raw materials for the product freely and plentifully available? Is there a scarcity of the raw material leading to competitive bidding with the attendant danger of the price rising? And water and power?
3. ***The investment:*** How much is the investment? How soon can the machinery be obtained? What is the cost and how much time it will take?
4. ***The Time Frame:*** How much time it will take from the day of the go-ahead to the time the project starts functioning, divided into the following:
   - *(a)* Land acquisition
   - *(b)* Obtaining various licences
   - *(c)* Machinery acquisition
   - *(d)* Sales organization

Table-5 is a sample of Feasibility Report

Table 5. – Feasibility Report

Date	August 22, 2006
To	Project Director
From	Feasibility study team
Subject	Setting up of a factory to manufacture glazed tiles to feed the Ghaziabad-NOIDA Marketing Territory

Study Team's Report

The Market: The Ghaziabad-NOIDA Marketing Territory, which is the project's target area, consumed 100,000 glazed tiles in fiscal 2000-2001, up from 91,000 in 1999-2000 and 82,000 in 1998-1999. The annual increase is about 10%.

Half the demand in fiscal 2000-2001 was met by our Delhi office which then controlled the Delhi-Ghaziabad-NOIDA-Gurgaon marketing territory. The other half was met by three competing companies which had their plants in Delhi.

With the eviction of industries in Delhi's residential areas, these three plants were relocated to Alwar, which is 250 km from Ghaziabad. Our company, which had been supplying the demand of the present territory plus Delhi from its plant in Alwar, decided to start a plant in the NOIDA Industrial Area with a separate marketing office in Ghaziabad for the Ghaziabad-NOIDA territory.

With our plant in NOIDA, the company will be able to supply the demand quicker and more economically than our competitors.

The Input: 100 kilolitres of raw water per day and a 5 KW power load have been assured by the NOIDA Industrial Authority which has issued the necessary clearances (attached). The raw material will be available from three cement plants in NOIDA which have undertaken to start supplies from January 1, 2007 (attached).

1. Investment

Fixed costs: Industrial plots admeasuring 500 sq. m. will be auctioned on Sept 20, reserve price Rs. 2.5 lakhs. At last auction such plots went for Rs. 2.70 lakhs to Rs. 3 lakhs. Area of 500 sq. m. sufficient to instal 1-lakh capacity tiles plant plus godowns to store raw material and 50,000 units finished product. Est. construction cost @ Rs. 200/ sq. ft.

for 2000 sq. ft.	= Rs. 4 lakhs
Cost of machinery	= Rs. 3 lakhs
Miscellaneous	= Rs. 1 lakhs
Total	= Rs. 8 lakhs

Working Capital: Cost of raw material stockpile	= Rs. 50,000
Water and power (per month)	= Rs. 5,000
Miscellaneous	= Rs. 50,000

Time Frame: (1) Bidding for land auction on Sept 20, possession on Nov 1. Construction time for factory and godown – two months; (2) no-objection certificate, if applied for now, by December 2; (3) If machinery ordered now, delivery at site by – December 15; (4) If civil works over by Feb 15, trial run for 15 days. Commercial production from March 15.

SUMMING UP

It is part of management to make many kinds of reports in upward vertical communication. There are routine reports and non-routine reports. Routine reports are of two kinds.

(A) *Production reports*—These are reports made by teams of field workers at regular intervals so that the top management can keep track of the working of the enterprise. If the organization manufactures, or assembles, or imports or exports goods, the production report sent periodically shows how much production was made. If it is sales, the report gives data about sales.

Similarly about imports and exports. Sales (or imports or exports) reports are also usually called production reports because commercial organizations are concerned with the production of value, whether through manufacture, sale, imports or exports.

(B) *Progress reports*—Teams commissioned with the erection of new plants or expansion of existing plants, or expanding the spread of the market, etc., make periodical reports. But they may be discontinued after the commission given to the team is completed. After trial the expanded production capacity or market becomes subject to the norm of filing production reports.

Progress reports, apart from specifying the progress made, also tell about the problems encountered and how they were overcome. Also worth telling is how and in what time frame the rest of the work of the team can be completed. Usually there is a fixed format to follow.

There are some other kinds of reports:

A. Interview reports are submitted by a man or a team commissioned to interview consumers, retailers, etc., to find out their preferences as between different alternatives. Apart from reporting the data, they analyze them and report their conclusions as recommendations.

B. Feasibility reports are filed by individuals or teams commissioned to investigate whether a sales or production facility needs to be established. That is, whether it is feasible to establish it. Feasibility reports are usually made under the following heads:

(a) The size of the market.

(b) The input required.

(c) The investments required.

(d) The time frame.

Self-Check Exercises

1. Describe the differences between a production report and a progress report.

   (Space for answer)

2. List the four heads under which a feasibility report is made.

(Space for answer)

18

Non-Routine and Special Reports

We have discussed how there are routine reports filed to carry on the business of an organization. Among them the most common are production reports. One kind can be the routine reporting of the physical production made by the company or by a particular unit of it. This business report is filed periodically so that those in charge of the running of the organization can keep track of whatever is going on.

Apart from physical production, such reports are filed also for marketing or sales. They are also filed periodically as a matter of routine so that the marketing of its products or services can be monitored.

There are, then, reports of the progress of various projects embarked upon by the organization. They are called progress reports and are filed periodically, or when asked for, so long as the project lasts. For instance, a company may want to set up a new production or sales unit. From the start the man or team commissioned to set up the project will go on filing progress reports until the project has been set up. Then regular production reports for it start being filed so that those in charge of the running of the company can monitor the new unit's performance.

Cartons or Bags

There are, then, other reports. For instance, a company carrying on the business of supplying spices to a particular market may carry out a survey to find out whether consumers prefer spices packed in cartons or in bags. This is usually done through interviews or by making consumers fill out a questionnaire. The data thus collected are collated and analyzed to decide which mode of packaging is preferable. For such interviews interview reports are filed, collated and analyzed.

Another form of report is called feasibility report. Such reports are made after finding out various facts, such as the availability of raw materials, the extent of the market, the degree of competition, the cost involved, etc. A feasibility report is usually commissioned when it has been decided to set up a factory or a sales unit and the only question is its location, the size, the area to be covered, etc.

In rare cases, where the feasibility report is very disappointing, that is, when it shows that the setting up of the proposed unit is just not feasible, the project may be given up. If, however, it is decided to persist with the project, a person or a team is commissioned to set it up. This person or team starts sending periodical progress reports.

Special Reports

There occur events in an organization's life when it is necessary to commission special reports. A unit of the organization may report awful results, or may persistently give unexpectedly disappointing results. The top controlling body or person of the organization, such as the Managing Director or the Board of Directors, may commission such a fact-finding study, which is usually required to make its recommendations for action to be taken to remedy the situation.

As an example, when the Varanasi edition of the *Pioneer* daily of Lucknow did abysmally from the time it was started in 1984, the Managing Director, Shishir jaipuria, decided to send me, the daily's Deputy Editor, to find out what was wrong with it.

This is because the Editor of the daily, R D Kwatra, had been of opinion from the time of the launch of the Varanasi edition that the Resident Editor was no good. The Resident Editor was, in his turn, of opinion that the Editor was no good. Faced with the mutual condemnation of each other by the Editor and the Resident Editor, Shishir decided on me to find the truth out.

There were Three Reasons

(*a*) I had earlier in my career worked as a junior to Kwatra and he had in fact handpicked me to join the paper as his Deputy Editor and prospective successor.

(*b*) I had likewise worked in a very senior position with the person who was now Resident Editor of the paper in Varansi.

(*c*) I had participated both in the remoulding of the Lucknow edition and in producing the Varanasi edtion's launch supplement which turned out to be far superior to the supplement produced by the Resident Editor in Varanasi.

The report on the Varanasi edition I was commissioned to make was a special report. In the normal course it was the Resident Editor who sent production reports periodically. But in the special situation in which all efforts to shore up the edition had proved futile, I was handpicked to make a special report.

Fourth Reason

I was handpicked for the three reasons stated above. A fourth reason was that, even though sitting in Lucknow, I had started a weekly column for the Varanasi edition named *Among Ourselves by Adarsh Banarasi*. I was able to write it because I had spent 13 of my growing years – from age 4 to age 17–in that holy city and knew the place, the people and the habits well.

One piece of this column talked of the bad habit of the people wasting time gossiping at *paan* shops. I had cited the example of Kabir, Tulsidas and other distinguished persons. All of them belonged to Varanasi but none of them was known to have gossiped at *paan* shops. If they had, they wouldn't have produced the voluminous and classy literature that they had.

This column, and specially the *paan* shop piece, had proved to be hugely popular in the holy city. This seemed to show to the Managing Director that I had an inkling to the kind of thing which would be popular in Varanasi.

In cases where special reports are commissioned, it is common sense to commission only those who have an inkling to the likely remedy to the problem.

If it has to do with sales, an expert or a team of experts in sales will be commissioned. But not those involved on a day to day basis in the problem area, for they would be familiar with the hurdles and pitfalls. A fresh mind is needed to evaluate the problem and find a solution. Even people outside the organization can be involved.

Times of India Case

Here is one more example from my experience. When the *Times of India* had only two editions, Delhi in the north and Mumbai in the west, it carried out a study to find out why the Delhi edition which fed Lucknow and other areas of U.P. could not make a dent in the local papers' circulation and advertising. The finding was that the Delhi edition had two handicaps in Lucknow.

First, the paper reached Lucknow after 7 in the morning. Hawkers by then would be out on their rounds in the city and would not be able to come back, pick up copies and deliver them to readers before 11 a.m.

The second handicap was that Lucknow being the capital of U.P., readers wanted much more of it in their morning daily than a Delhi paper could give. That is why there was no dent in the sales of the local papers–the *National Herald*, the *Pionner* and the *Northern India Patrika*.

Lucknow Edition

When the *Times of India's* Lucknow edition was launched, it overcame both these handicaps, and ate into the circulation of the local papers. Panicking at this, the *Pionner* spread the word that it required a senior journalist to blunt the thrust of the *Time of India's* Lucknow edition. That's how I came to be recruited as the *Pionner's* Deputy Editior. My role was to assist the Editor, Mr. R D Kwatra, for one year and to learn from him how the paper was run and then succeed him as Editor.

I studied the dent the *Times of India's* Lucknow edition was making in the *Pioneer's* circulation and advertising. I noticed that while the *Pioneer* was marginally ahead in local reporting and substantially ahead in reporting from nearby urban areas like Bara Banki, Rae Bareli and Amethi, it suffered in political reporting from Delhi.

While the *Times of India* had a full-fledged bureau in Delhi of two dozen special correspondents and a dozen or more staff reporters, the *Pioneer* was making do with two retired special correspondents who had been employed on cut-rate salaries to save money.

Remedy Prescribed

The remedy I prescribed was, to begin with, to strengthen the Delhi bureau by appointing at least two young and dynamic special correspondents. This was done and that's how Manoj Raghuvanshi came to be appointed the Delhi bureau chief of the *Pioneer*.

The long-term remedy was to start a Delhi edition of the *Pioneer* with a full–fledged bureau rivaling the *Times of India's* in numbers and quality. The Delhi edition of the

Pioneer which you now see is the result of that recommendation.

Special reports can relate to production and may, therefore, be called "special production reports", or to new projects and thus may be called "special progress reports" or to the feasibility of a proposal and may be called "special feasibility report" – like the one which gave birth to the Delhi edition of the *Pioneer*.

SUMMING UP

A special report is filed by a team or individual commissioned to report on an unforeseen development – why and how it took place,what is the remedy, etc. The team or individual commissioned has to be a specialist, if necessary from outside the organisation.

Self-Check Exercises

1. In what situation are special reports needed?

   (Space for answer)

2. Give an example from your experience of a special report.

   (Space for answer)

19

Some Characteristics of Business Reports

There are five major kinds of flaws which creep in into Business Reports. Consequently the business manager or executive should keep track of five characteristics, which a Business Report should have.

Accuracy: Every Business Report should be accurate and precise. By this it is not meant that 3 should not be typed as 5. That is not inaccuracy but carelessness. Look at this example, which actually happened in a notice for a meeting, which was scheduled.

The production staff will meet at 8 on Monday

This is an incomplete, and therefore inaccurate, notice, though it is sincerely intended to be an adequate notice. At 8 when, morning or evening? And which Monday, September 1 or September 8? Finally, where are the people to assemble for the meeting? Each one is left to guess. Some may decide that the meeting is to be held in the Production Manager's Office, others that it will be in the lawn where some meetings are occasionally held, and still others that the venue will be the conference hall. The accurate notice will therefore be –

The production staff will meet in the conference hall at 8 a.m. on Monday September 1.

Completeness: It is common among laymen to put things vaguely. For instance,

Production has declined by 10% during recent months.

It is not clear which are the recent months, the two months immediately past, or the three months or four months immediately past. The competent and careful manager will specify which months are "recent months".

Also, it is not clear whether the 10% decline has taken place over each of the recent months or over the whole of the period which is described as "recent months". The complete way of saying things would be –

Production declined by 10% in July over June and again by 10% in August over July.

Or, it can be that *production declined by 10% in September over the production in August which was the same as in July.*

It is also possible that production in September was 10% less than the combined production of July and August. The whole idea is to put things so clearly and completely that no questions are left to be asked.

Clarity: A famous *mantra* repeatedly chanted by professionals of all disciplines including management goes as follows:

Management *Mantra* 3 for Professionals

In mass communication, the more simple word / expression / sentence structure replaces the less simple.

Some examples will make things clear.

Less clear : Please return the questionnaire as soon as possible. Your comments will be valuable.

Clearer but not clear enough : Please fill up the questionnaire and return it by September 1. Your answers will help us decide.

Clear: Please fill up the questionnaire and send it so that it reaches us by 5 p.m. on September 1. Your answers will help us decide whether to keep the weekly bank holiday or open the bank all days of the week.

This makes it clear that filling up the questionnaire by September 1 is not good enough. It is necessary for it to reach its destination by 5 p.m. on September 1. Further, it makes it clear how the answers will help and what they will help decide.

The golden rule is that the simple language with a subject, a verb and a predicate is the most preferable. It leaves very little to imagine. For instance :

Complex, to be avoid: That Ram is a good boy is known to everyone.

Simple and therefore preferable. Everyone knows that Ram is a good boy.

Complex and avoidable : Because there was insufficient evidence, he was acquitted.

Simple and therefore preferable: He was acquitted because of insufficient evidence.

Confusing Statements: A very frequent *mistake* committed in business communication is the use of the same pronoun for different persons or things leaving the recipient confused to whom or what it refers. Sample the following:

He made it clear that if he absented himself the next day he would suspend him.

Note the first "he" refers to the speaker, the second to the listener, the third to the speaker again and the final "him" back to the listener. It should be obvious that once "he" is used for one of the parties, no other party should be referred to by the same pronoun in the same sentence. Yet it is common to find people get trapped in this pitfall. It can be done easily if only a little attention is paid to this need. Here it is reworded–

The manager made it clear to him that if he absented himself the next day he would be suspended.

Here "he" and "himself" refer to the same person wherever they occur.

There is also a tendency to confuse issues similarly by making it difficult to understand what is meant. Sample the following from a business message written by a counter clerk to his manager:

Note from counter clerk to manager: *The couple came on the way to an evening party, spent time choosing, and wanted delivery at home.*

This note leaves the manager guessing whether the couple wanted the merchandise delivered at home while they were at the evening party or whether they wanted it delivered when they returned home. Why leave the manager guessing? He could immediately send the commodity to the customer's home, or wait until he thought or found out that the couple had returned home.

Yet another pitfall lies in reciting the whole sequence of events or conversation but leaving out the operative part. A shop assistant at a furniture dealer's sent a note to the manager saying the husband wanted the standard height for the chair and table, the wife wanted the table to have rounded corners and the child wanted both the table and the chair to be four inches less in height since he was short in stature.

Now, what is the manager to do? It was good of the assistant to be attentive to the desires of the customers, but in his enthusiasm for detail he forgot which table and chair the family wanted, or if he did find this out he forgot to inform the manager which set to pack for delivery, so excited he was by the exchanges with the customer family.

It is not uncommon for families to visit shops only to find several items attractive but with funds which cannot buy all of them. Customers being customers, each member of the family will plump for his choice. But while empathizing with customers, the shop assistant can help resolve the inconsistencies by suggesting ways out of the dilemma. If the shop's policy allows this, he may indeed suggest part payment by post-dated cheque. But there is no scope for ambiguity.

Structural Consistency

It is important to have structural consistency, specially in a Production Report, Progress Report, or Feasibility Report. Savour the following which occurred in a statements comparing the Feasibility Report and the Production Report for the same project.

Feasibility Report		*Production Report*	
Land acquisition	Rs. 20 Lakhs	Cost of land	Rs. 35 Lakhs
Civil Works	Rs. 22 Lakhs	Construction cost	Rs. 23 Lakhs
Light & Power	Rs. 7 Lakhs	Power connection	Rs. 7 Lakhs
Cement, limestone	Rs. 7 Lakhs	Raw material	Rs. 7 Lakhs
Capital Expenses	Rs. 56 Lakhs	Start-up cost	Rs. 72 Lakhs

Logical Consistency

The need for logical consistency arises in analyzing the data that have been collected. For instance, you advertise to recruit five business executives each capable of procuring orders for 10,000 glazed tiles a month. There are 30 applications, so you report this fact to the Managing Director and add "we are on the brink of doubling sales from 50,000 to 100,000 tiles a month."

Is the conclusion right? Supposing you find only two applicants willing to make the great effort and only one of them has the capability to sell 10,000 tiles. Your report to the Managing Director will be premature, to put it mildly.

The analysis of the data has not been logical. All that you should have reported is that "it will be only after interviewing them that we will be able to say how many of them will be willing to sell and capable of selling 10,000 tiles a month."

Give Reasons

When analyzing data for the big boss, it is necessary to give reasons why you have arrived at your conclusion. He will then be able to evaluate whether your conclusion is justified.

In rejecting a quotation, instead of saying "your quotation is unacceptable in its present form", it more prudent to say what is wrong with the "present form", and even more importantly, to say which alternative form will be acceptable. So, instead of rejecting the quotation with the above wording, better write "your quotation does not mentioned whether cartage is or is not included".

In fact, it will be better still if you ask for this clarification so that a decision can be taken whether a business deal is possible. Always remember that you are in the market to make a deal, not to find fault with others or to teach them how to make a quotation. This is the demand of the market.

Remember in this context the distinction that we made among interpersonal transactions, official-business business transactions and business-business business transactions. In both the first and third cases the intent of both parties is to make a transaction. It is only in the second case, that is in the official- business business, that one of the parties is more interested in the procedure than in the transaction itself. That is the official party, for whom a transaction is only the outcome of following the prescribed procedure, not the goal of conducting business.

It is important for all management students to learn that the end result of the efforts of all professional managers has to be the transaction of business. Those who do not keep this uppermost in their minds and think that holding down the job is all that matters can never succeed.

Holding down the job is for the unambitious. Those who have the ambition to be successful in business have to aspire to accomplish the transaction of business.

SUMMING UP

There are certain characteristics which have to be there in special reports. They are being specified here because the characteristics of routine and non-routine reports have already been specified where they are discussed.

1. Accuracy 2. Completeness 3. Clarity, simplicity 4. Non-confusing statements 5. Structural consistency 6. Logical consistency.

Self-Check Exercises

1. Described what completeness of a business report means.

   (Space for answer)

2. Why should business reports be couched in simple terms? Give an example.

   (Space for answer)

20

Answers to Self-Check Exercises

Part 1 : A Symbiotic Relationship

Chapter 1 – Crusoe, His Man Friday and The Message of The Gun

1. It is an organization in which leave cannot be availed of unless it is sanctioned. Since no sanction has been received, he cannot go on leave. In this case silence itself is the message that leave has not been sanctioned.

2. Master: "Dinner should be ready when I return at 9 p.m."

   Servant: "I want to see my sister now. It will be 9.30 p.m. when I return."

   No reply.

Chapter 2 – Vertical and Horizontal, Upward and Downward Communication

1. Vertical communication can be from the top management to the lower levels of management and usually consists of orders and information. This is downward communication.

   It is upward communication when it goes from lower levels of management to higher levels and usually consists of production and/or progress reports, accompanied sometimes by suggestions and/or requests.

2. Cluster communication is downwards, usually consisting of an order or directive to junior managers. An example is an order/directive from the Superintendent of Police to all police stations.

Chapter 3 – Process of Communication: The Role of Encoding

1. The process of communication begins with the communicator. He decides what message to communicate, codes it in such a way that it is easily and accurately understood, and then transmits it.

   The receiver receives the message and decodes it. He then decides his response, codes and transmits it back. This is called feedback.

   The communicator receives the feedback and decodes it.

2. When my four-year-old son started going to school in July 1968, he returned everyday exhausted at 2 p.m. and wanted to lie down, but his mother would hand him a glass of cold drink, undress him and push him into the bathroom. The cold drink and the undressing were the code. The message was that he must wash and eat before resting.

Chapter 4 – The Art of Listening and Decoding

1. One kind of distraction to listening is an unconnected sound, like a knock on the door or the blowing of a whistle. A second kind is to let the mind wander, for instance to think of the clever remark you made to a friend earlier in the day. A third kind of distraction,

more common, is to start formulating a response before the communicator has completed giving the message.

2. Catch words or phrases which a communicator uses are a peg to convey his message. *The Buddha Is Smiling* was the phrase used by Dr. Raja Ramanna to convey the message to Mrs. Gandhi that India's first nuclear test at Pokharan in 1974 was successful.

   If a speaker tells a public meeting that *the Rajasthan desert is dotted with the carcasses of cattle,* the message is that Rajasthan is experiencing an acute shortage of water and fodder.

Chapter 5 – Time Management and Fixing Priorities

1. Everyone has 24 hours at his disposal. But all the tasks he has to do during the day are not equally important. Which means the person must decide how much of his 24 hours can be devoted to which task to get the most important of the tasks done and which task can be dropped or postponed in order to get the maximum satisfaction from the day's exertions.

2. Prioritization is necessary so that the most important of the tasks are not left undone. If one does not fix priorities, it is possible that the less important tasks get done while some of the more important ones remain to be done or are done unsatisfactorily in a hurry.

Chapter 6 – Image-Building and the Making of a Brand

1. An image is the picture that appears in the mind of the qualities, positive or negative, of a man or a company. A positive image is one of quality, reliability, punctuality, etc. A negative image means lack of trustworthiness.

2. The image is the picture a name creates on the brain of a product or service. If a series of products bearing

the same name create a picture on the brain of the same kind of reliability, durability and quality, the name becomes a brand.

Examples – Siemens for electronic and electrical appliances.

Glaxo for pharmaceutical products.

Chapter 7 – Brands have Cash Value, can be Sold and Bought

1. A brand is an unwritten promise of the quality and performance of a particular branded commodity or service. Since quality and performance vary from brand to brand, so does the money value.

2. When one pays a fee or royalty for using a brand, it is a transaction of the sale of a services or intellectual property. Hence it attracts service tax.

   When a franchisee uses a well-known brand name to enhance the appeal of its goods or services to charge a higher price, it attracts VAT since the use of the brand name adds to value.

Chapter 8 – Crucial Role of Vision in Management

1. Vision is the capability to know what one wants to happen. Only when one has vision can he employ management techniques like persistence and mental virility to make it happen.

2. The major contribution of Dhirubhai Ambani to the development of entrepreneurial culture was to promote the equity cult in India. Another major contribution was that growth could be made possible only by increasing volumes of business.

Chapter 9 – Different Patterns of Communication

1. JRD Tata made the Tata brand strong, enduring and diversified. Under him, each company of his group

was headed by a satrap who was fastidiously trained and briefed to produce the best product most competitively. After this, the communication was mostly between the Chairman of Tata Sons Ltd. and each individual satrap. This proved fruitful so long as JRD Tata was at the helm.

2. Buddhadeb Bhattacharya's communication to investors was that "there is something for you here." Business would be able to thrive without undue demands or gherao by CPM cadres or workers' unions controlled by them.

Chapter 10 – Dhirubhai Ambani Pattern of Communication

1. Dhirubhai Ambani was fired by the entrepreneurial spirit. Despite earning a comfortable living in Aden, he returned to India to start an enterprise like Burmah-Shell. Once he told an associate, "...... the excitement is to build. *Usme nasha hai*".

2. Dhirubhai was routinely denied capital by banks started by the Government to promote industrial development. So in 1977 he floated an IPO (Initial Public Offering). It was subscribed. Promptly he declared a dividend of 15 per cent. Next year's dividend was 27 per cent. The year after, there was a dividend of 25 per cent plus a 3:5 issue of bonus shares. In the next three years he issued partly convertible debentures. The policy of handsomely rewarding investors consistently led to the creation of the world's "largest family of shareholders."

Chapter 11 – Hero Group's Multi-tier Communication Model

1. The Hero Group's multi–tier communication model involved two major things. First, the management

suo moto arranged for a series of ancillary industries and widespread distrubtion of products which meant easy availability of quality spare parts. Second, the management kept its ear to the ground to know what the customer wanted and quickly provided it.

2. The production of scooters was licensed to only two parties in the early 60s. Since more licenses were not issued and production was limited, sales were no problem. Consequently there was no need to improve and update technology. When motor-cycles came, they had vastly improved technology, better fuel efficiency and muffled noise. Secondly, Hero Honda came with the reputation of being a macho product.

Chapter 12 – Positioning and Other Subtle Management Tools

1. Positioning is the strategy of occupying a place in the consumer's mind which sets your brand apart. It gives the brand a distinctness that attracts a given consumer segment.

2. Television soap, as pioneered in Peru and used in Mexico and India, brings education in wholesome social values through entertainment. The entertainment attracts the audience and the wholesome messages sink in.

Chapter 13 – Marcom or Marketing Communication: Final Management Tool

1. Marcom or marketing communication is necessary to complete the management process since, without it, the value produced doesn't reach the consumer – production is stillborn, distribution is futile and consumer awareness is useless.

2. Advertising is like fishing. You cast your net without aiming at any particular catch. Public relations is

aimed at the image- building of an organization, and acting is imitating real life situations and actions, actual or supposed, with or without a message. Marketing is aimed at a carefully selected audience to tell it why going for a particular product is good for it.

Chapter 14 – Five Mandatory Communication Mantras of Management

1. He cannot scale down quantity or quality. Though the price was scaled down during negotiations, the quantity and quality were not.

2. This is not a good business communication since the party giving the order cannot be certain when the tiles will be delivered. The transaction may be cancelled.

3. This is the correct response, but if the order specified where to deliver the goods, the response should commit the supplier to deliver at the place specified.

Chapter 15 – Some Norms for the Usage of words and Expressions

1. (a) India, along with South Africa and Sri Lanka, is to participate in a triangular ODI series.

   (b) India, South Africa and Sri Lanka are to participate in a triangular ODI series.

2. Many thanks for your order of five lakh glazed yellow bathrooms tiles.

Part 2: Business Communication

Chapter 16 – Different Kinds of Business Communication

1. I will agree to the delivery of 70,000 yellow tiles on the seventh day, with the remainder to follow two

days later. The reason is that not all the one lakh tiles can be used in one day. While the 70,000 tiles are being utilized, the remaining 30,000 will come.

2. Business is not the Government's business, since all Government work has to be done according to a prescribed procedure. Business, on the other hand, is concerned with being transacted in a time frame, following any procedure provided it is not illegal.

Chapter 17 – Production, Progress and Other Reports

1. The production report describes the production done, whether of the physical product or of sales. The progress report describes the progress made in the setting up of a new plant or the expansion of an existing one.

2. The four heads under which a Feasibility Report is made are –

   (a) The size of the market.

   (b) The input required.

   (c) The investment required.

   (d) The time frame.

Chapter 18 – Non-Routine and Special Reports

1. Special reports are commissioned when routine reports are not able to pinpoint the faultiness in a production unit. Usually people unconnected with the production unit are commissioned to make such reports.

2. When the Lucknow edition of the *Times of India* was started, the local daily, the *Pioneer*, started losing circulation to it. A special report was commissioned, and the recommendations were, first, to strengthen the Delhi bureau and , second, to start a Delhi edition of the Lucknow daily.

Chapter 19 – Some Characteristics of Business Reports

1. Completeness means that the report should specify the time frame, fix targets, etc.

2. "Simple terms" means that the report should be understandable at first glance and should not require a second look.

GUEST CHAPTERS

Guest Chapter 1:
A Karma Yogi Who Lived the Gita

By Anil Ambani

July 6 will always be an emotional day for the entire Ambani family. It is my father Dhirubhai Ambani's Nirvan Divas.

Many knew him as a visionary who created a business empire and became a legend in his own lifetime. But few are aware of the spiritual underpinning to his material achievements. I once asked him: "Do you read the Gita?" He replied: "I live the Gita".

In the Gita, Parthasarathi tells Arjuna: "No one has attained his goal without action... if even I were to cease working, the world would perish. How much more necessary then for the people at large to engage in action?"

My father, a god-fearing and family loving man, who believed in Karma and its effects, took Lord Krishna's wisdom to heart as a valuable lesson. But the fruits of his labour – success for his corporation and wealth for the nation – never changed his value system. He used to say: "Whatever you do, be down to earth, be humble and be simple. Humility in success is the best virtue to have."

He never wanted anything for himself. When I asked him what he missed not having, he would reply, "education". He wanted to study, but did not have the resources. He made up for that more than adequately by ensuring that my brother, two sisters and I got the best education. Yet, I feel that with his education in the school of life, and insatiable thirst for knowledge, he was always two steps ahead of all of us.

He was the simplest of men. He dressed in a white shirt, navy blue trousers, black belt, black shoes, and blue socks. His everyday wardrobe contained six such sets. That was enough for my father.

He didn't revel in fame. What he revelled in was doing things. On every achievement, whether major or minor, he would be jubilant. He would take a deep breath, smile with satisfaction, and say: "Growth is life". He would be overjoyed that Reliance's 33 lakh shareholders had something more to be happy about, and that more wealth had been created, making India a stronger country.

And then, just so none of us got the wrong idea about achievement, he would reiterate – as he did so often: "Our dreams have to be bigger, our ambitions higher, our commitment deeper, and our efforts greater. This is my dream for India."

On July 6, 2002, his personal physician, Dr. Pandey, told me, "Sir is a person who will not inconvenience anybody. If he goes, it will be on Saturday night, after the day's work. The funeral will be on Sunday. It will be over by evening, and on Monday morning, everyone can get back to work."

My father passed away at 11.50 p.m. on Saturday night. The funeral was on Sunday. On Monday morning, we were all back in office. My father, who believed work is worship, would not have wanted it any other way.

I came home at 2.30 a.m. the night my father passed away. I woke up at 5 a.m. and went to tell my mother. She saw my face, folded her hands and asked: "Did he go peacefully?" I said yes, "he had a big smile."

Seeing my grief, she told me: "Your father has gone to heaven – that is his permanent home. God sent him to earth on a mission. He chose India, and he chose this family. Now there are others to carry on his mission here, so God needs him back in heaven to do His work."

It was a mother's way of comforting her son. She also did it to convey the message that her husband would want life to go on.

MEMOS FOR MANAGEMENT

Guest Chapter 2:
When Less Is More

By Gurcharan Das

Soon after he became prime minister, Winston Churchill wrote to the head of the British navy to say, *Pray Sir, tell me on one side of one sheet of paper, how the Royal Navy is preparing for the war.* Churchill knew that if he did not qualify his request he would receive an unreadable 400-page report. Brevity is a great virtue, but nowhere more than in the world of action–in business, politics, and war – where one has to communicate clearly, briefly and boldly. Hence, Abraham Lincoln's Gettysburg address is only 212 words long, and it is one the great speeches in history. The Lord's Prayer is only 78 words, but the European Economic Commission's report on the import of caramel is 17,400 unworthy pages.

We Indians are verbose, and need to be reminded that human beings were born with two ears and two eyes, but with only one tongue, so that we should see and and hear twice as much as we say. Our judges write judgements that are too long; our lawyers ramble on; our executives try to impress with lengthy memos; our politicians – well, try to get in a word. Our public affairs would improve tangibly if our power to be silent were equal to our power to speak.

That less can be more is especially true in good writing. I discovered this in Procter and Gamble, a company as famous for its legendary one-page memo as its products. Its wondrous one-page memo was created out of the same confidence in reason and technology that built America, and is as elegent as Panini's grammar or Euclid's geometry. Based on the reasonable assumption that all managers suffer from an overload of paperwork and files, it is simple, factual, and logical; the reader scans it in minutes, grasps its contents, and comes to a decision. It has just enough data that a manager needs to make a decision and no more. It is clear, precise, eschews hyperbole, and it actually improves the speed and quality of decisions, and hence is a source of competitive advantage.

The one-page memo generally consists of five or six short paragraphs. Its first sentence tells the reader what to expect – why should you be interested in what I have to say? Hence, the smart writer puts his best foot forward and states upfront the conclusion or recommendation. There is an inherent conflict between the reader and the writer's interests, for the writer wants to build a case slowly, leading to a conclusion, but the busy reader wants to quickly get to the conclusion (and is only interested in the rationale after that). Remember, this is not a detective story, and a good first paragraph ought to focus on the *what* and not the *how*; but it must, of course, offer one or two reasons to believe in the recommendation.

The second paragraph offers beckground – it is historical, factual, filled with data, and tells the reader why the problem or opportunity has arisen. The third para is the detailed recommendation – the what and the how, but don't confuse the reader here with the why. The rationale comes in the next paragraph – here are three reasons why you should accept my recommendation – and typically cites precedents, benefits (financial and otherwise) and risks. The fifth paragraph tells the reader that I have looked at alternative courses of action, and why this is the best. The last paragraph addresses the next steps and lays out a plan of action that will flow from the decision.

What I have said here might apply to any business letter and the Maharashtra Administrative Reforms Commission is so impressed with it that it is thinking of recommending it to the government to make bureaucrats efficient. Shakespeare too, I think, had Indians in mind when he wrote in *Richard III*: Talkers are no good doers; so, he offered us this advice in *Henry V*: Men of a few words are the best of men.

Index